Becoming Autistic

Becoming Autistic

How Technology is Altering the Minds of the Next Generation

Dr Rachael Sharman & Dr Michael C. Nagel

Copyright © Rachael Sharman and Michael C. Nagel 2022

All rights reserved. No part of this book may be reproduced or transmitted in any form or by any means, electronic or mechanical, including photocopying, recording or by any information storage and retrieval system, without prior permission in writing from the publisher.

Published by Amba Press
Melbourne, Australia
www.ambapress.com.au

Editor – Pauline Hopkins
Cover Designer – Alissa Dinallo

Printed by IngramSpark

ISBN: 9781922607140 (pbk)
ISBN: 9781922607157 (ebk)

A catalogue record for this book is available from the National Library of Australia.

To Laura, for keeping me sane and humble and motivating me to be a better version of myself each and every day. – Mike

To children, who are our future. – Rachael

Contents

List of Illustrations	ix
Acknowledgements	xi
About the Authors	xiii
Introduction: What's Happening to Young Minds?	1
Chapter 1: Imagining the Unimaginable	9
Chapter 2: This is the Brain on Adolescence!	23
Chapter 3: Entering the Matrix	37
Chapter 4: The Divine Glow of Screens!	53
Chapter 5: The Usual Suspects: Violence, Addiction, Cyberbullying and Cybersex	65
Chapter 6: Social Media or Social Disease – The Girls Are Not All Right	77
Chapter 7: Autistification of a Generation	87
Chapter 8: Get Out and Get Real – Nature as a Buffer to All Things Virtual	99
Conclusion: Be Concerned and Vigilant, But Not Afraid!	111
Chapter Notes	115
Bibliography	121
Index	133

List of Illustrations

Figure 1. Brain stem and cerebellum　　　　　　　　　　　12
Figure 2. The limbic system　　　　　　　　　　　　　　13
Figure 3. Cerebrum　　　　　　　　　　　　　　　　　　14
Figure 4. Neuron with myelin sheath around axon　　　　　17
Figure 5. Amygdala and nucleus accumbens in limbic system　31

Acknowledgements

Comparatively speaking, writing a book is much easier than being a parent. Both of us can speak from experience and we think it only fitting to acknowledge all those parents who do their best to raise happy and healthy children. There isn't a magic bullet or one-size-fits-all model for being a parent and there will always be ups and downs ... to that end we hope this book offers you some solace in knowing you are not alone and some guidance on how you might make things better when it comes to supporting children in a rapidly changing technological world.

We'd also like to acknowledge all of the inspirational researchers and scholars we have drawn upon to help shape our research, thoughts and writing. Relatedly, it would be remiss of us not to acknowledge the support of our university and all those at the University of the Sunshine Coast that we call friends and colleagues.

Finally, if not for the people of Amba Press this book would still just be a collection of ideas on paper. A huge thank you to Alicia Cohen for her support, guidance and unyielding faith in this project and a resounding thank you to Pauline Hopkins for her meticulous editorial work and for giving our words and ideas greater clarity.

About the Authors

Dr Rachael Sharman is a senior lecturer and researcher in psychology at the University of the Sunshine Coast, specialising in child and adolescent development.

Dr Sharman's research is focused on the optimal and healthy development of the paediatric brain and she has published over 30 peer reviewed journal articles and two book chapters. Dr Sharman is a volume editor for *The Encyclopedia of Child and Adolescent Development* and a special issue editor for the *International Journal of Environmental Research and Public Health*.

Dr Sharman is an enthusiastic and engaging public speaker with a weekly guest spot on ABC radio, and has had articles published in various newspapers, *Time* magazine and on the *The Conversation* online. She has appeared as an expert guest on television including on The Project and SBS Insight.

Dr Michael Nagel is an Associate Professor, teacher and academic at the University of the Sunshine Coast, in the areas of cognition and learning, human development and early learning, neurological development in children and adolescent psychology. He is regarded as one of Australia's foremost experts in child development.

With decades of experience as teacher and behavioural specialist on multiple continents, Dr Nagel has written numerous books and articles related to neurological development in children and is a feature writer for the *Child* series of magazines, which offers parenting advice to more than one million Australian readers. He is a member of the prestigious International Neuropsychological Society and is a national and international speaker.

What's Happening to Young Minds?

"The great danger we face as we become more intimately involved with our computers – as we come to experience more of our lives through the disembodied symbols flickering across our screens – is that we'll begin to lose our humanness, to sacrifice the very qualities that separate us from machines."

— Nicholas Carr[1]

We were born and raised in different times: one of us a Baby Boomer and the other the child of a Baby Boomer or a Gen Xer, depending on who you speak to. And while ten years separates us, the context of our childhoods is not too dissimilar. We grew up using a telephone with a cord strategically placed in the home, with televisions that were often constructed as a piece of furniture and with limited channels to view, and where almost all financial transactions occurred by cash or some form of cheque. Our news was seldom fake and not always timely. Events happening on the other side of the planet were not always available in real time or 24/7. Board games were something families enjoyed together, game show prizes were limited to home appliances or, if generous, to a car. Computer games were only beginning to emerge. Compared to today, our childhood and teenage years seem to be light years behind us, for the devices we found in science fiction books, television shows or movies are now held in the palms of our hands or on the drawing boards of companies in Silicon Valley. Importantly, the boundaries between defining human and machine are becoming increasingly blurred as technology continues to make inroads into our lives. It is our contention that such inroads, or shall we say intrusions, are altering the minds of 21st century young people in ways we are only beginning to understand.

Since the turn of the century there has been a great deal of research exploring how technology and the internet might be impacting on the brain. This has been complemented by research examining the impact of screen devices on many aspects of child and adolescent development. Everything from attention to concentration to physical health to psychological wellbeing are increasingly scrutinised by researchers interested in the potential impact of a 'screen-driven' society on the bodies and minds of a species whose brain takes almost three decades to fully mature. Yes, three decades! The human brain is not fully developed until somewhere after our 23rd birthday and varies between males and females. This means that some of the most critical aspects of neurological development occur in children and teenagers. Moreover, this development is occurring in social, cultural and contextual environments that are vastly different from those experienced by any previous generation. At no point in the history of humanity has information and technology had such a pervasive impact on human development and, by most measures, the influence of technology and, by association, screen devices is only increasing. Therefore, we think that the ubiquitous nature of screen devices coupled with concerns around what such devices might be doing to young minds is a story worth telling. This story is not asking people to abandon screens, as that type of reductionist thinking is not realistic, but instead looks carefully at screen usage, especially by children and adolescents, and suggests that parents should apply a 'precautionary' mindset whenever they hand a device to their child. In other words, we posit that parents should consider the risks with engaging in screens and take caution in circumstances when the degree of uncertainty surrounding the outcomes of the risk is too high.[2] We will unpack that further throughout the book.

From the outset it is important to offer some insight into the thoughts and ideas that have helped shape the title of the book and the words you are reading now. To begin, we would argue that too often any discussion of screen devices, social media, gaming and tech use is dominated by individuals with a vested interest in promoting the use of technology, by politicians expounding soundbites of technology as a panacea for learning or by experts in media studies and/or 'e-learning' (electronic learning). To be clear, their expertise is not in child and adolescent development or health. For child development experts, psychologists and neuroscientists, it is not just the technology itself that is concerning us but also the content of young children's experiences with screen devices. This concern is not based on any hostility towards technology but purely on concerns surrounding the premature use or overuse of screens in young people whose brains and bodies are not yet fully formed. It is our contention that because of the pervasive nature of screens, and the taken-for-granted ubiquity of screen devices, we believe screen time must now be considered a major public health issue. Reducing screen time must become the new priority for child and adolescent health. Perhaps the most confronting reason for our position is the growing incidence of perfectly 'normal' children displaying autistic-like behaviours, which appears to be linked to screen usage. This is particularly evident in the stories and examples provided in the chapters you are about to read.

Chapter 1 provides some basic understanding of the human brain and how it develops. It tells the story of how the brain, or the most unimaginable thing imaginable,[3] starts as a few cells in utero to become one of the most complex structures in our universe. Of most importance in this chapter is the explanation of how the brain can change and how experiences can impact on brain development. This is referred to as 'neuroplasticity'. While a malleable brain offers humans a range of evolutionary and survival advantages, it also makes it very susceptible to unwanted alterations.

The next chapter then focuses on the developing adolescent brain. Many people might not be aware that while a 15-year-old might look like an adult in terms of physical stature, the gelatinous mass between a teen's ears is going through a major reconstruction. The developing adolescent brain is not a miniature adult brain and it might actually influence its owner to do things that would defy logic or belief in the eyes of most. In terms of maturation, adolescent development goes well beyond reproductive changes, hormones and acne. The adolescent brain is in the midst of a myriad of changes that will impact on most aspects of behaviour and this in turn is also influenced by the environment and context. The key message here is to consider what is happening to a developing adolescent brain and, by association, mind, when it is spending a large amount of time staring into a screen. There are also questions to be answered in terms of what happens to an adolescent when they are bombarded by unwanted pixelated images, malicious content, disingenuous individuals or any range of things from which previous generations of parents could more easily shield their children.

Chapter 3 offers insights into the rapid changes that occurred in technology and computers leading into the 21st century and the subsequent advances that have taken place at an unprecedented pace or what we refer to as The Matrix, premised on the motion picture. The information age, along with advances in technology, has changed our lives in many ways but some of those changes and their purported advancements have received little scrutiny. Couple such rapid changes with the understanding that it has taken thousands of years for the human brain to evolve into the marvel it is and it should be evident that too much too soon, in terms of immersing a young mind for extended periods into a virtual world, may not be all that positive in the long term. We would like to give you, the reader, a different and arguably more informed perspective while suggesting that you take *the red pill!* The red pill is a purposeful reference to *The Matrix* film trilogy ... if you haven't seen the movies, the red pill refers to your willingness to learn potentially unsettling or life-changing truths.

Chapter 4 then takes us further into The Matrix by scrutinising the omitted, unspoken or hidden issues shining through the divine glow of screens – what screens do to very important aspects of children's and adolescents' innate physical and psychological functions. This then offers a foundation for Chapter 5, which teases out the ever-increasing evidence of problems that arise when screen usage overlaps with violent media, addiction, bullying and pornography.

Chapter 6 furthers our journey of unsettling truths by focusing on how social media might more aptly be described as a social disease. Yes, it sounds extreme, and while we acknowledge the existence of some benefits for connecting with others online, we also think it important to present evidence indicating that social media is a major contributor to a wide array of psychological disorders that, prior to the beginning of the 21st century, were actually less evident or even in a state of decline. From the moment we were huddled around our televisions watching our clocks move from 1999 to 2000 while waiting for the world to end because of Y2K, the mental health of young people has declined precipitously. And this at a time when, by most measures, life has improved for people around the globe.

Chapter 7 then gets to the heart of the matter by looking at how screens can rapidly diminish our social skill set. Human beings are, by nature, social beings and it is our contention that screens are contributing to the 'autistification' of a generation. Borrowing from the work of evolutionary biologists Heather Heying and Bret Weinstein, we posit that screen usage is producing what we call 'contextual autism.'[4] This is what sets our work apart from others who have looked at the downside of screens and screen time. We contend that, based on the evidence, screen usage with all of its inherent apps and benefits is so focused on bombarding the developing brain with sensory data, that little or no importance is given to its impact on emotional and social development. For thousands of years the human brain has evolved in a milieu of social interaction in real time and this is being displaced by a virtual world that is numbing our children's senses.

And finally, Chapter 8 provides some idea of what can be done to buffer the impact of screen usage and to help ensure your children do not lose themselves in their own little virtual worlds. It turns out that the solution to healthy development and overall wellbeing can be found not far beyond your front door. So while screens are here to stay, your children do not need to get lost in The Matrix but instead can find all they need in the real world if you give them chances to do so.

We were born and raised in different times and the times, indeed, are a changing. We are not advocating a romanticised view of history and a call to return to days gone by at the expense of advancements that have improved our lives. Instead, we contend that it is important to be informed consumers about the issues surrounding the very products that influence and inform our children's lives. A screen device is a tool with many uses but we want to show you that it can also be an instrument of social and emotional harm if left unchecked, or at least without some guidelines around usage and balance in relation to other important aspects of growing up. The fundamental message of this book is simple: think about the time your child or teen spends on screens and ensure that they are spending more time doing other things, especially if they can do so outdoors.

Your Child's Developing Brain

"Where society once viewed the child's brain as static and unchangeable, experts today see it as a highly dynamic organ that feeds on stimulation and experience and responds with the flourishing of branching, intertwined neural forests."

— Marian Diamond and Janet Hopson[1]

Imagining the Unimaginable

Close your eyes for a few seconds and think of a human brain and then continue reading when you grow tired or bored of that task. During that process of thought we are quite confident that your mindful meanderings were likely confined to thinking about the brain's shape and in particular its two hemispheres. This is not a criticism but rather a simple statement of fact – most people can imagine the shape of a brain but actually know very little about it. Even scientists who spend their lives studying the brain would likely agree that they know very little about the gelatinous universe between our ears. Neuroscientist and author Joseph LeDoux has even gone so far as to suggest that the human brain is so complex that it is best described as the most unimaginable thing imaginable.[2] However, difficult as it may be for us to fully understand the brain, there are some things that we do know that are important for parents and anyone who works with young people to know. In this chapter we provide a necessary foundation for understanding how the brain matures, works and can be shaped.

First, let's start with some basics. A mature brain is about the size of a coconut and weighs roughly one and a half kilograms. In itself, the brain is a massive collection of nerve cells, which consist primarily of glial cells and neurons that act together as a system for gathering information from the environment and transferring that information to regions of the brain where it is needed. This passing of information is performed via electro-chemical impulses between neurons – processes more commonly referred to as synapses – and is aided by various neurotransmitters, or chemical messengers. Neurotransmitters, in turn, play an important role in most everything we do and as such are noted throughout much of this book ... let's continue!

At birth, the brain has far more neurons than it needs but relatively little connectivity between those neurons. Over the first few years of life, a child's brain will grow to become a neural superhighway of connectivity via experiences from the environment. The brain is literally shaped by experience.

By the time a child is blowing out the candles on their third birthday cake, their brain has been so busy soaking up life's experiences that she or he will actually have more neural connections than their paediatrician's brain. You see, the brain overcompensates and develops more connections than necessary but modifies itself during adolescence. There is more on the beguiling topic of the adolescent brain to come later, but now that you have some understanding of the building blocks of the brain, it is time to look at certain structures and functions.

Structures of the Brain and for the Mind

As alluded to earlier, whenever anyone thinks of the brain they generally have an image of the overall brain and its two hemispheres. The brain actually has three significant regions with a number of important structures in each. While we might like to break the brain up into three sections for discussion purposes, all of those sections are intimately connected and rely on one another to operate efficiently. That being said, each region does maintain some primary roles in all that we are and all that we do and the first of these is the brain stem.

Nestled at the base of the brain, the brain stem is a collection of structures that connects the spinal cord to the brain. Most people know that physical trauma to the neck can lead to forms of paralysis but may not be aware that damage to regions of the brain stem can also be life threatening. Aside from the brain stem's role in controlling vomiting, sneezing and coughing, it also ensures that your breathing, cardiac rhythm and blood pressure are functioning properly.[3] The brain stem is also our primary survival centre. When we are threatened, it is the brain stem that tells the rest of the brain and body to be alert and prepare to run as quickly as possible or stand our ground and battle – what is more commonly known as our 'fight-or-flight' response. And finally, there is one other important structure that sits just above the brain stem worthy of mention: the cerebellum.

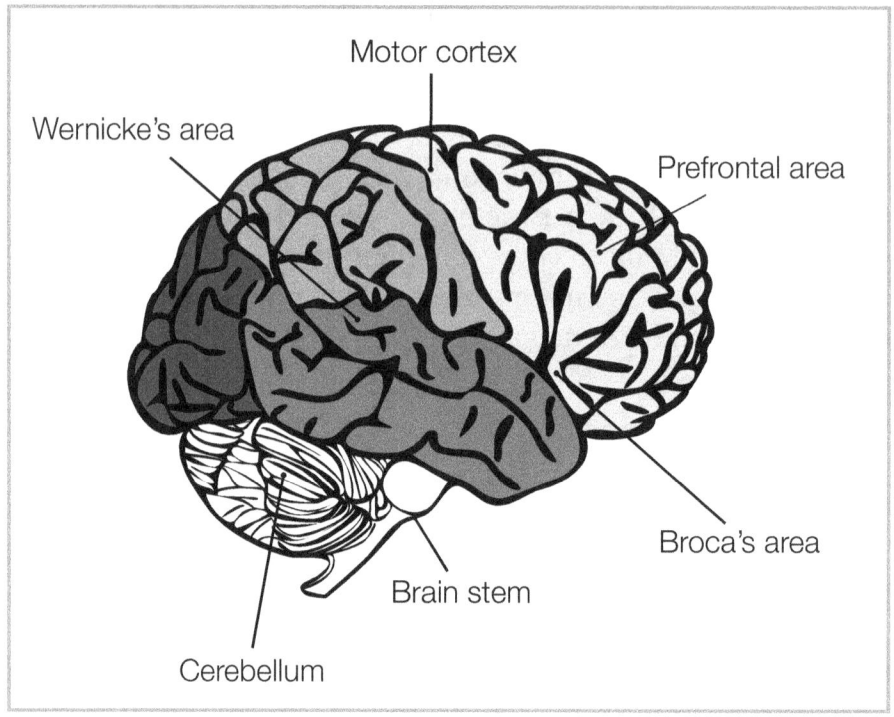

Figure 1. Brain stem and cerebellum

The cerebellum, a word aptly derived from Latin and meaning 'little brain', houses about 50% of the brain's neurons.[4] This complex structure is a good example of the interconnective nature of the human brain due to the fact that it plays a role in not only shaping our thoughts, but also moving our muscles. The cerebellum helps interpret and integrate sensory input, and coordinate our movements while also coordinating various cognitive (thinking) functions and processes.[5] Damage to the cerebellum can be far-reaching and lead to tremors, involuntary contraction of muscles, vertigo, and cognitive impairment, with some researchers suggesting links between cerebellum dysfunction and anxiety disorders, dyslexia, autism spectrum disorder (ASD) and schizophrenia.[6] So important and connected is the cerebellum to the rest of the brain that it can, when impaired or damaged, impact the limbic system and by association our emotions.[7]

Sitting above the brain stem and at the heart of the brain, pun intended, is our emotional centre or what is known in neuroscientific terms as the limbic system. This 'system' is actually a collection of structures that do a myriad of things but most notably process memories and emotions. By way of example, imagine an elephant. Now imagine that elephant to be in your favourite colour. Finally, while holding this image in your mind, have that elephant sing a song that makes you happy. If we were scanning your brain right now, we would see certain structures in your limbic system, and in particular the hippocampus, busy at work drawing experiences from your long term memories of pachyderms and linking them with your tune of choice. But wait, there's more!

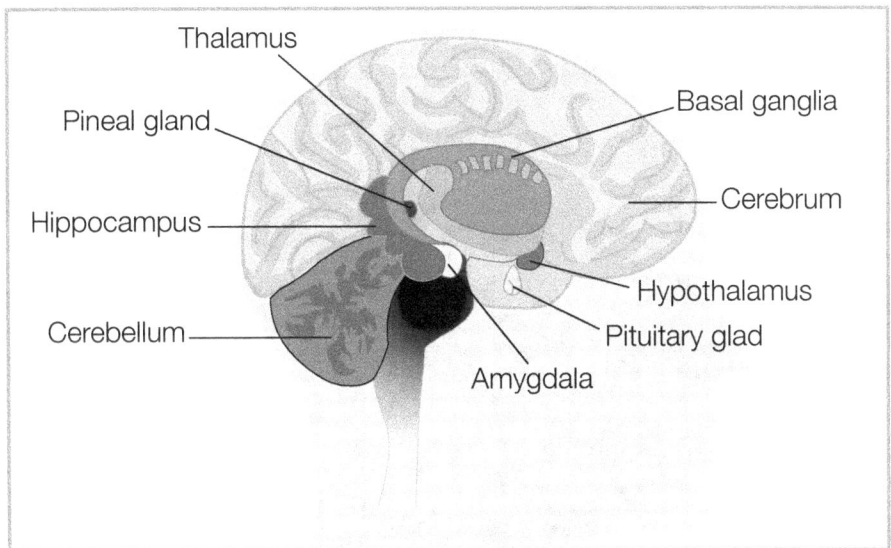

Figure 2. The limbic system

Although we tend to focus on the limbic system's role in memory and emotion, this important region processes environmental stimuli and plays a role in sleep patterns, attention, motivation, hormones, the regulation of bodily functions and the production of most of the chemicals in the brain and various other mechanisms that influence behaviour.[8] Are you impressed yet? If not, then it is also noteworthy that with all else that it does, the limbic system is an active influencer in many of the higher order thinking processes that occur in the cerebrum, or most advanced part of the human brain.

At the beginning of this chapter we asked you to think of a brain and suggested that you likely held the image of the brain's hemispheres in your mind. If this was indeed the case, then you were thinking of the cerebrum. This is the largest and topmost part of the brain, surrounded by a thin layer of specialised cells called the cerebral cortex and made up of two hemispheres. Each of these hemispheres is, in turn, comprised of four lobes: the parietal lobes (that manage sensory information like touch and temperature); the occipital lobes (that process visual information); the temporal lobes (that manage auditory information and the processing of some visual stimuli); and, most importantly, the frontal lobes (the CEO of the brain).

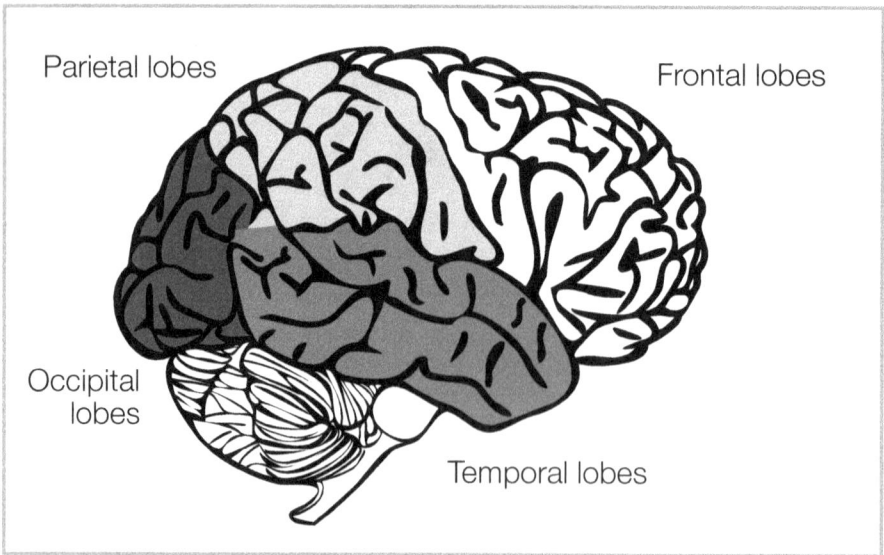

Figure 3. Cerebrum

There is no way to overemphasise the importance of the frontal lobes, for they are what effectively separates us from all other species on earth. Other mammals, including our primate cousins, have frontal lobes but they pale in aspects of size, function and ability when compared to humans. It is the frontal lobes, and in particular the prefrontal cortex, where higher order thinking occurs along with many of the things we take for granted: problem solving; attention; concentration; planning; empathy; decision-making; responsible thinking; judgement; emotional regulation and problem solving are but a few of the things that occur in the frontal lobes. For neuroscientists, it is easier to refer to all of these activities as 'executive functions' and the frontal lobes are indeed the brain's Chief Executive Officer. In terms of children, adolescents and overall development, there are some really important considerations regarding the frontal lobes that are worth mentioning.

First, and using computer terminology, the frontal lobes are not fully 'online' until we are in our mid-20s. Developmentally speaking, they are the last things to mature and do so earlier in females than males. For females most of the hard work towards development is completed around the age of 24, with some scientists suggesting a couple of years later for males.

Because it takes almost three decades for the brain to fully mature, there are some very good reasons why children have difficulty regulating their emotions and why adults often find themselves looking at teenagers in utter disbelief at choices made, or decisions taken. In Chapter 2 the developing adolescent brain is examined in greater detail but keep in mind that the analytical part of the brain can be at the mercy of the survival and emotional parts of the brain long after children and teens finish school. Equally significant is realising that the most important region of the most important organ in the body is the last thing that fully develops and as such is continually influenced and shaped by the environment.

Experiences Matter!

Earlier in the chapter it was noted that experiences shape the brain; our brains come prewired but they need stimulation to become hardwired.[9] Recall that at birth we have very few neural connections but with each day the environment and the people in it provide a vast range of experiences which help build our neural connectivity and, by association, our minds. It is also noteworthy that the types of experiences we are referring two can actually be split into two categories – experience-expectant and experience-dependent stimulation. We would argue that rather than trying to remember those terms, maybe think of them as nature and nurture.

Experience-expectant stimulation refers to the everyday experiences we, as adults, take for granted and do not think about too much. For example, you are able to read these words because your visual system and all its neural complexity was developed early in life when your eyes started to take in information from the environment. At birth, our visual system is rudimentary in design and efficacy or, simply stated, we are not good at seeing things. Each day, however, as we take in visual stimulation and as an important material called myelin grows and expands, the neurocircuitry for sight develops. A quick word about myelin is appropriate here.

Myelin is a white fatty material, often referred to as the white matter of the brain, that grows in fits and starts in different regions of the brain and at different times. It will increase more than 100% during adolescence and the brain is not fully myelinated until we are well into our third decade of life. Its importance lies in the fact that this fatty material helps with the transmission of information from one neuron to the other. Myelin grows and wraps around the axons of a neuron (see diagram on facing page) and acts as an insulator and conductor, much like plastic around copper wire. The more myelin we have the better and its importance is evident in the fact that it is myelin that breaks down in those who suffer with multiple sclerosis. In terms of experience-expectant growth, the brain expects certain things to happen, like seeing things in the environment, and as it does so in conjunction with myelin growth, our senses and brain systems become more acute and function optimally.

One final word about experience-expectant growth is that barring any physical impairments or extreme deprivation of stimulation, the everyday experiences of life will provide what is needed for much of our neural hardwiring. It also wondrously appears that children enter the world prewired for certain abilities that unfold as long as the brain receives the stimulation it expects.[10] However, deprive the brain of certain experiences through trauma and/or neglect and you are setting up a child for an array of developmental problems including cognitive deficits, attention difficulties, behavioural problems and a myriad of other socio-emotional issues. In other words, early life experiences, or the lack thereof, cause differences in later abilities and behaviour.

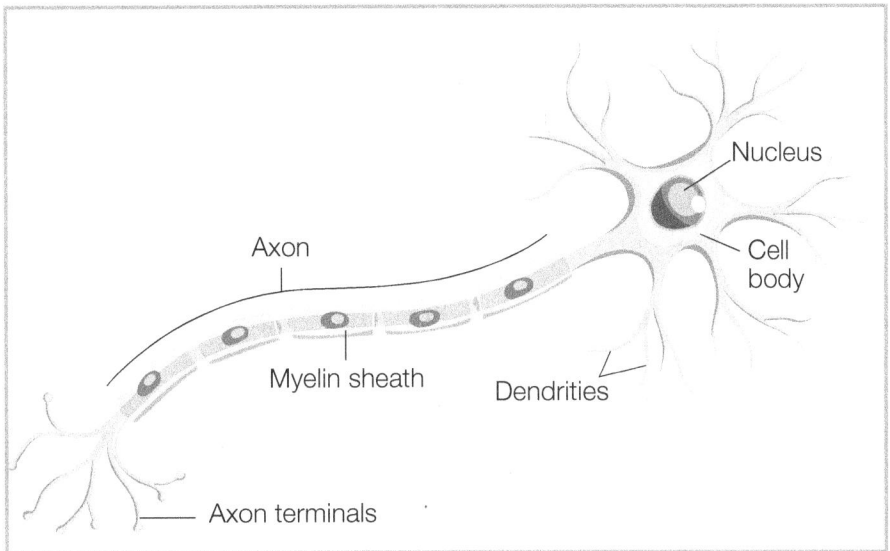

Figure 4. Neuron with myelin sheath around axon

Now that you have a sense of experience-expectant development and its links to myelin, let's talk experience-dependent development or 'nurture'. In its simplest sense, experience-dependent development occurs through those experiences that are provided to us by the people and events around us. You could just as easily call it learning as well as nurture. For example, when we model how to hold a spoon to an infant, and they in turn practice doing so, their brain is busy making connections en route to making such an action occur without much conscious thought or effort. The more they practice, the better they get at it over time, and the less thinking and effort needed in the future for such a mundane task.

In other words, what we do to, and with, children matters, given how immature their brains are and how malleable and plastic they are as they grow and develop.

The plasticity of the brain is very important in terms of experiences but before exploring neuroplasticity there are some final points regarding the types of experiences discussed earlier that are worth noting. First, while experiences are indeed important it is also pertinent to remember that no two brains are the same and there will be variations in individual development even when the environment is the same. Most parents will attest to the fact that their own children are very different. This is because many traits and characteristics are better predicted by children's biological relatives rather than the environment. Autism, dyslexia, many learning disabilities, left-handedness and bipolar illness, for example, are hereditary and not programmed by the environment.[11]

Second, it should be apparent that experience-expectant development is a universal process that applies to all children. Provide visual stimulation to any child at birth regardless of culture or context and the brain hardwires for sight. Experience-dependent processes, on the other hand, are more individualistic given they are specific learning experiences with specific people in specific contexts. In the end, experiences are important given that they literally shape the brain and by association the mind.

And finally, while some might think that if experiences are so important in terms of brain development, then the more experiences the better, this is a very problematic view. Trying to somehow hyper-stimulate development by increasing the quantity of experiences fails to take into account that the human brain has its own timelines in terms of all aspects of development. Pushing things onto children before they are developmentally ready can lead to a vast array of problems and should be avoided. It is the quality of experience that matters, not the volume. This is linked to myelin as noted earlier and neuroplasticity as discussed next.

Neuroplasticity or the Brain's Ability to Change

Arguably, most people have heard about the brain being 'plastic' or some reference to 'plasticity'. Not so long ago, however, the brain was thought to be mostly unchangeable with a specified number of brain cells and neural circuits. In fact, it was believed that any changes that occurred were due to loss of cells or some form of trauma-related damage. We now know that the brain is indeed rather malleable and some things can change in a heartbeat, some over time and some not at all depending on age. Such changes are usually discussed under the broad umbrella term 'neuroplasticity', which refers to the brain's ability to change, modify and adapt functions and/or structures throughout life and in response to the environment.[12]

In order to best understand brain development and plasticity, especially in terms of the impact of technology on the brain, there are three things we would like you to know and remember. First, the brain's main job throughout childhood and adolescence is to change itself.[13] If you recall from the beginning of this chapter, at birth a child's brain has billions of neurons that are busily making connections with one another via stimulation from the environment. As we get older, weaker connections are pruned away, predominantly during adolescence, while stronger connections are maintained and strengthened. This process allows for the brain to become more efficient and work faster. The development and pruning of synaptic connections as a process of adaptation is one example of the brain's neuroplasticity. Importantly, the more permanent neural pathways beyond adolescence never really stop adjusting. When we engage in new or novel activities, when we learn something or when we commit things to memory, our neural pathways are altered to accommodate such events. However, some aspects of neuroplasticity are not so accommodating. This is best understood through the next two interrelated things we want to unveil to change your brain and can be summed up as 'silly putty' and 'cement'. Allow us to explain.

As noted earlier, brain maturation is more marathon than sprint. The brain is primed for experience, and experiences matter. At birth the brain is very malleable or plastic and can be moulded, like silly putty, by those experiences. The more that those experiences occur or are practiced, the firmer that silly putty becomes. A not-so-scientific-sounding adage often used to explain this is 'use it or lose it'. Neural hardwiring depends on repetition and practice and at no time is this more evident than in early childhood and adolescence. Remember that early in life, the brain actually has more connections than necessary and these are shaped on a developmental timeline by, and with, the environment. During adolescence, the brain starts getting rid of unused connections to become more efficient and expedient in how it processes information. During these times, using it or losing it is a very apt phrase. Again, we will explore the adolescent brain in more detail in the next chapter but let's pull things together by moving from silly putty to concrete.

Let's begin by emphasising that the brain can change in response to the environment. Throughout our lives our brains are very plastic and can change in an instant. For example, think of a time when you were startled by the unexpected bark of a dog. Chances are you may have jumped a little, your heart rate might have increased, you may have gotten goosebumps, you may have let out a yelp or a scream or you may have even broken into a sweat. During that event, your brain would have been busy trying to work out what was going on and deciding if you should freeze, fight or flee. There would have also been changes to many neurons in your brain as they responded to the perceived threat at hand and, in that fleeting moment, your brain went through measurable change. Being scared to death actually changed your brain. Indeed, your brain changes when you watch a movie, meet new people, when you practice your tennis serve, when you read the words on this page – quite simply it changes "whenever an experience leaves a trace in the mind."[14] For neuroscientist and author Dr David Eagleman, the brain is probably best considered as being 'livewired' given it is a "dynamic, adaptable, information-seeking system."[15] In terms of thinking about neuroplasticity, that is a wet cement version of concrete but there is a more set version of concrete as well.

While our brains are capable of change throughout our lives, there are things that gain a degree of permanency as we age. A fully developed adult brain is less able to recover from trauma compared to the young brain of a child. As the years pass, some aspects of our neural circuitry and the structures housing them become less malleable. The case of Jody Miller provides a great example of this.

Jody was born in 1990 and, not long after birth, her parents noticed something was wrong. Jody was suffering from a rare condition called Rasmussen's encephalitis, which was wreaking havoc in the right hemisphere of her brain. This rare inflammatory neurological disease causes severe seizures, loss of motor skills and speech, weakness on one side of the body, encephalitis and can lead to dementia-like behaviours. The disease generally occurs in children under the age of 15 and, in Jody's case, at three years of age she was dealing with an increasing frequency of life-threatening seizures, which led to severe paralysis on the left side of her body. (The human brain is contralateral, meaning that the right hemisphere controls the left side of the body and vice versa.) Over time the seizures Jody was having were getting worse and not responding to any treatment so the only choice the doctors felt they had was to perform a 'hemispherectomy'.[16] A hemispherectomy, in layperson's terms, means that neurosurgeons completely removed the right hemisphere of Jody's brain, with unforeseen and, dare we say, miraculous results.

Unsure about what to expect or how to measure any degree of success, the surgeons were surprised to find her seizures ended and she recovered very well. While there were some minor post-operative challenges that were treated with physiotherapy, Jody Miller survived and has grown into adulthood, graduated from college, received many scholarships and awards and is living a normal life, all with only half a brain. You see, it turns out that Jody's left hemisphere took on the roles vacated by the right hemisphere – an amazing sign of neuroplasticity if ever there was one. To date, multiple children have undergone successful hemispherectomies and experienced the brain's miraculous ability to self-heal, reconnect its neural network, and enable a normal life. However, there is an important caveat to those, and to Jody's story. A key factor in the likelihood of a successful outcome after removing half a person's brain is age. It is unlikely that if such a procedure were performed on an adult the results would be equally successful. With age comes a degree of permanence and, like the timing from when wet cement sets, dries and hardens, there are age limits to aspects of the plastic nature of the brain. Relatedly, the younger the brain the more susceptible it is to environmental influence and one of the most critical times where this can occur is when puberty kicks in and your children may become something you find hard to comprehend. The next chapter helps to explain why this is so.

This is the Brain on Adolescence!

"Adolescence, the interval between the onset of sexual maturation and the attainment of adulthood, is a time of dramatic changes. The long-held idea that human development is virtually complete within the first few years of life is a serious misconception. Many aspects of brain maturation continue throughout childhood and well into the late teenage years."

— Ronald Dahl[1]

Adolescent Anecdote!

We thought we might open this chapter with a personal anecdote. These sorts of things act as a reminder that all of us have gone through adolescence and been through 'dramatic' changes. Sometimes, adults spend too much time lamenting the youth of today while conveniently forgetting they too were imperfect human beings when puberty kicked in.

One of us – Michael – grew up in the prairies of Canada with a younger sister and brother and two working-class parents. Mum was a short-order cook and while she worked part-time most of her life, she also worked hard at home raising three children. Dad was a blue-collar steel worker. Like many previous generations of parents, he worked for the same company for most of his life, for almost forty years until he retired. Dad was a BIG man … literally! He stood about six foot two (1.88 metres) and his German ancestry afforded him a rather large bodily frame that could provide shade from the heat when I was a small child. His hands were the kind of appendages that could make things vanish when he held them and his arms were powerfully built and menacing during a time when parental discipline might mean a smack on the bottom more often than not. Such was the man I called Dad. I can still vividly remember a time when I was 14 years old and found myself in a state of complete bewilderment and fear. Imagine the following if you will, as a fly on the wall.

It's dinnertime and we are all gathering at the table to eat. My dad has just returned home from work with a weary face lightly dusted with remnants of his day. As he approaches the table to sit, the telephone rings. For those perhaps too young to remember, this was a time when mobile technology and cordless phones did not exist, and our phone was in the kitchen within reach of everyone and everything. I leapt out of my chair to grab the phone and beat my sister to it. I did manage to beat my sister to the receiver and hoped it would be one of my friends or, better yet, the girl down the street who I had only just discovered. It was indeed a friend and as we began chatting, my adolescent brain prompted me to do the unthinkable. As my dad went to sit down at the table ... I pulled the chair out from under him.

Pulling the chair out from under someone when they are sitting down is not an uncommon prank between classmates and a sure-fire way to get a laugh from one's friends. Pulling the chair out from a six-foot-two, 220-pound tired steelworker you call 'Dad' is something completely different. He hit the floor – hard! My eight-year-old brother stared in disbelief and my 12-year-old sister's face displayed messages of inner delight knowing what I was in for. My mum stood there, literally in shock, and as my dad began to get to his feet I could see her trying to work out how she might protect her eldest cub while she scanned his unpleasant and unfolding posture. I quickly said goodbye to my friend, hoping it would not be the last time we ever spoke, and hung up the phone. My body tightened in fear and anxiety due to my dad's icy stare as he bellowed out a question many parents and teachers have used for generations: "Why on earth would you do that?" My empty frontal lobes could only muster up the following: "I don't know!"

We think that it's a safe assumption that most of you have asked the question or perhaps even had to answer it! Too often adults forget that they went through adolescence as they bemoan or decry the youth of the day. They may also not reveal how their own indiscretions from the onset of puberty through the teen years shape their decision-making when it comes to their own children, with such discretions remaining hidden for as long as humanly possible. Such is often the nature of being an adolescent and then an adult. But what is it that might propel an adolescent to do things that make a younger sibling cringe in absolute disbelief? It turns out there are several substantive changes that are invisible and unmatched by the physical changes that become increasingly evident as sex hormones start doing the job of transitioning the body of child into that of an adult.

The changes associated with hormones and adolescence were characterised at the turn of the 20th century by one of psychology's founding fathers, G. Stanley Hall, to be "suggestive of some ancient period of storm and stress."[2] Even Aristotle had his views on this time of life and quipped that youth "are heated by Nature as drunken men by wine."[3] Fortunately, advances in neuroscience and technology tell us that any storm or stress or heating of youth is attributable to much more than hormones. There are some significant developmental changes in the brain that also play a significant role when it comes to understanding adolescent cognition and emotions and, by association, behaviour.

Prior to looking at some of these changes a bit of context is prudent. First, we would argue that it is important to remember that developmental changes in the brain are not isolated to the teen years. However, changes to the brain begin before the age of 13 and continue beyond one's 19th birthday. To simplify things, we use the term 'adolescent brain' but acknowledge that most of the substantive changes occur somewhere between 11 and 19 years of age with some fine-tuning afterwards.

Secondly, while adolescence can indeed be a time of storm and stress, many adolescents navigate this storm with minimal difficulties so it's best not to over-generalise and assume all adolescents are the same. Yes, some will display greater anxiety or stress than others, which can impact on their wellbeing, relationships, education and future. Many more will get along well with others most of the time, succeed in school and life, become healthy productive adults and not fall into a pit of delinquency.[4] It is noteworthy, however, that for those adolescents who struggle, screen devices can exacerbate the challenges they face or be a contributing factor. Chapters 3 and 6 delve into this in much greater detail so for now let's return to the adolescent brain.

The adolescent brain is under massive reconstruction and is a work in progress as alluded to with the timelines earlier. This remodelling of some of its basic structures can impact on those mechanisms and regions responsible for everything from logic and language to impulses and intuition. So substantive are these changes that they have provided enough material for whole volumes of work on the topic, which go beyond what we need to do here. Instead we will focus on some of the most significant changes that, in turn, might help you understand why your happy eight-year-old may have morphed into an emotionally charged, sensation-seeking creature who often resembles a character from apocalyptic zombie movie due to sleep deprivation and task avoidance disorder (not a medically recognised diagnosable disorder, just our way of remembering our own children). The best place to start is with the brain's CEO!

Dude! Where Are My Frontal Lobes?

"Why on earth would you do that?" Asking an adolescent that question is an adult's first mistake. Expecting an answer or some form of explanation is the second. The reasons for such assertions are that, quite simply, the adolescent brain is an immature version of the adult brain and asking the question and expecting a reply is often doomed from the beginning. This has been touched upon earlier, but the emphasis is worth the repetition ... an adolescent brain is still under development. Perhaps nowhere is this more evident than in the brain's frontal lobes, and in particular, the right prefrontal cortex.

The previous chapter offered some initial insights into the monumentally important structures of the brain known as the frontal lobes. It is the frontal lobes that separate us from all other species of life and this region is arguably the epicentre of the mind. Decision-making, responsible thinking, planning, anticipation, attention, concentration, analysis, empathy, sequencing, learning from errors and various other higher-order thinking skills all reside in, or are a part of, the brain's frontal lobes. Damage to this region of the brain can lead to untold consequences and influence everything from temperament to judgement to personality to, well you're getting the picture, almost everything that makes us human.

The frontal lobes, and in particular the prefrontal lobes, are also the last regions of the brain to reach maturity, do so earlier in females and are significant mediators in helping to channel and harness the seething energy of the emotions within the limbic system. It is the prefrontal lobes that reach out to guide other parts of the brain including the regions that govern motivation, emotion and rewards. Immature prefrontal lobes in adolescents result in them being hotwired for emotional, risky, sensation-seeking behaviour but too often unable to think through the consequences of their actions.

It is noteworthy that brain scans show that an adolescent's brain literally looks different from that of a child or adult. The fact the frontal lobes do not appear adult-like is practically evident in any issue concerning teenagers including voting, drug use, risk taking, sexual behaviour and screen time.[5] According to neuroscientist and author Professor Frances E. Jensen, the adolescent brain is not just an adult brain with fewer miles on it, it is in essence a different kind of brain altogether.[6] This is not to say that adolescents should be excused for less than desirable behaviour but rather viewed in the knowledge that their frontal lobes are in a state of transformation. It's also a truism that consistently making good decisions is not always a reasonable expectation of a mature adult brain so perhaps some measure of understanding and empathy is warranted when adolescents make a bad choice like pulling the chair out from under a parent. A related example of this can be found when we consider Theory of Mind.

I Know What You're Thinking!

Imagine this... out of the corner of your eye you see a family member looking into the refrigerator and immediately deduce that that person is hungry. You call out to them that there are some leftovers on the bottom shelf or that there are biscuits in the cupboard that they might like. What you have done is exercise a basic aspect of Theory of Mind (ToM).

ToM is the ability to think about what another person is thinking or, in more colloquial terms, the ability to put yourself in another person's shoes. This important aspect of social cognition not only includes the ability to understand and predict another person's mental processes, including their emotions, thoughts, intentions, beliefs and motives, but also permits us to think about our own mental state.[7] ToM gives us a crucial evolutionary advantage over all other species in that it allows us to better interact with the environment and cooperate more efficiently with others.[8] In the context of this book, it is noteworthy to know that the emergence of ToM is, to date, somewhat contentious. However, there is evidence to suggest that it does not appear to be present at birth, seems to emerge around four or five years of age and adolescents do not appear to have a ToM as fully developed as that of adults.[9] Theoretically, this makes sense, given that most of the hard work for effectively thinking about your own mental state or the thoughts and feelings of others likely relies a great deal on activity in the frontal lobes. It seems self-evident that ToM would require a sophisticated relationship between the brain's CEO and its emotional heart. In other words, in order to be socially effective and have a fully functioning theory of mind, one must have a degree of control over, and a capacity for, integrating the full range of thinking and emotional processes.[10] For adolescents, this may not be something easily done given that their brains are still maturing and as such, perspective taking, reading social cues and other aspects of ToM may not be up to par for a period of time. Never forget, there is a great deal going on in the brains of adolescents, which, in turn, impacts on all aspects of the mind.

Their Changing Mind!

You may be wondering at this stage what exactly is going on in terms of overall maturation of the adolescent brain that can impact on most measures of thinking and behaviour. The story behind this is multi-layered, worthy of careful consideration and starts with the white fatty material known as myelin discussed in the previous chapter. If you recall, myelin is the material that wraps around the axons of neurons to aid in the transmission of messages from one neuron to the next. During adolescence it will increase about 100% and as an adolescent grows to become a 'fathead', the messages in the brain travel faster and with greater proficiency. Bear in mind we are talking milliseconds in spite of the blank gaze you may encounter when questioning an adolescent's motives or behaviour. And while there is the building up of myelin, there is also a state of deconstruction occurring as well.

It was noted in the previous chapter that the brain of an infant actually has more neurons than it needs and by age three has far more neural connections than the adults around it. During adolescence the brain then works to eliminate those connections linked to actions, activities and experiences no longer practiced or important and strengthen the connections that are repeatedly activated. This process is commonly referred to as synaptic pruning and neuroscientists use the technical phrase 'use it or lose it' to describe this journey of neural refinement. An important consideration here, and in the context of this book, is the role of the environment in helping shape an adolescent's neural superhighway. Using it or losing it relies on what an adolescent is doing and practising over this important time of development. Since the turn of the century, an increasing amount of time has been, and continues to be, spent with screens, online or connecting in a virtual world. The term 'screenager' comes to mind here given the amount of time adolescents spend engaging with the world though computers and smartphones. Worryingly, time on screens seems to be impacting the brains of young people in ways we are only beginning to understand ... more on that in later chapters.

Okay, so we have myelin increasing and synaptic connections decreasing. Of interest here also is that the brain matures roughly from the bottom (brain stem) to the top (cerebrum) and around to the front and in different areas and at a different rate for males and females. This is important given that regions and structures of the brain associated with rewards and emotions mature sooner than the frontal lobes, so thinking and behaviour can be impacted in various ways. Two such structures that might influence behaviour are the nucleus accumbens and the amygdala.

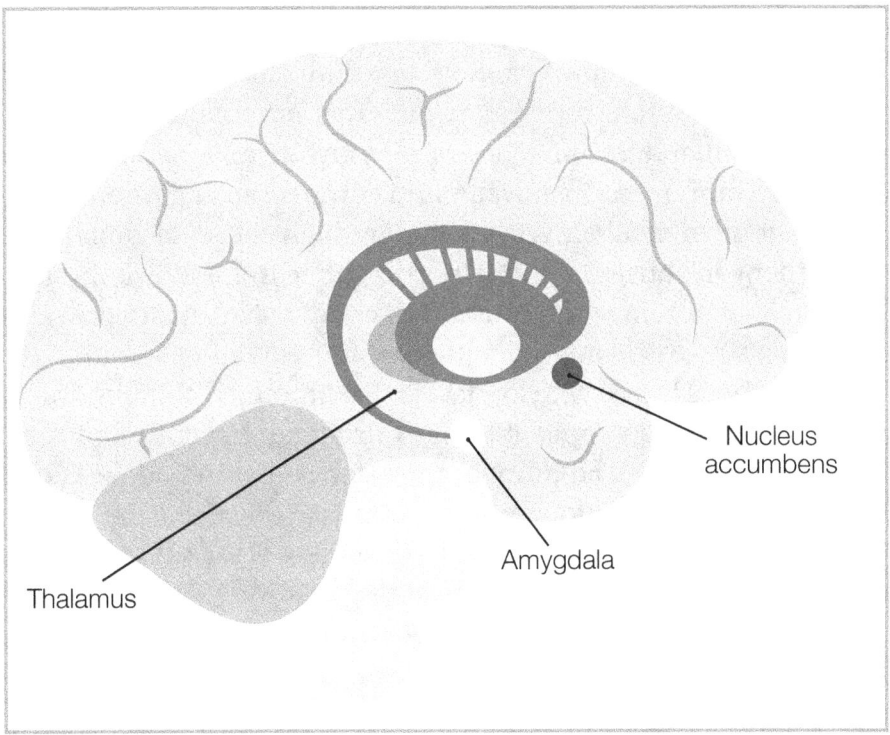

Figure 5. Amygdala and nucleus accumbens in limbic system

Hotwired for Emotion!

Arguably, one of the most primal drivers of human behaviour is pleasure seeking associated with rewards. Indeed, it is evident that every living thing is willing to expend a certain amount of effort in order to seek and receive rewards. World-renowned psychologists such as B. F. Skinner helped to demonstrate such behaviours in animals but humans will also seek out rewards and it is the nucleus accumbens that directs such behaviour. The nucleus accumbens is a central component of the limbic system found deep in the brain that is activated during pleasant or emotionally arousing experiences. It is a key player in the reward circuitry of the brain. Its operation is based on a couple of neurotransmitters, most notably dopamine, the chemical that promotes desire and pleasure, but also serotonin, which influences our sense of satiety, inhibition, calmness and wellbeing.

The role of dopamine cannot be understated in terms of understanding adolescent behaviour. This important chemical is much more than just a marker for pleasure given it appears to be a central component in novelty and reward seeking, motivation and feelings of wellbeing. Exceedingly high levels of dopamine are evident in those individuals who suffer from schizophrenia, Tourette's syndrome and obsessive-compulsive disorder while Parkinson's disease and difficulties with maintaining attention on tasks have been linked with low levels. The amount of this important neurochemical also appears to rise during adolescence and then begins to decline as adulthood approaches. During adolescence there seems to be a 'dopamine' power-play between the higher order, and yet still maturing, thinking regions of the brain, and the more primal emotive systems, resulting in responsible decision-making often giving way to impulsivity and risk-taking. In a cyclical fashion, risk-taking promotes increases in dopamine, which may predispose adolescents to further risk-taking. This is not to say that all adolescents will indulge in exceedingly risky behaviour, but many will, and changes in behaviour may be a manifestation of changes to dopamine levels, or other neurotransmitters and/or hormones.

Of further interest here is that during adolescence, receptors in the nucleus accumbens are engorged with dopamine but because the brain is still maturing there is often a disconnect between the effort expended and the desire for a reward. Adolescents tend to prefer activities that require relatively low to moderate effort yet produce immediate high rewards. This further exacerbates sensation-seeking and risk-taking behaviours ranging from playing video games to skateboarding to riding on the tops of trains to sexual behaviours to experimenting with alcohol and drugs. Sensation-seeking and risk-taking behaviours are important evolutionary drivers for becoming independent so should not be considered as wholly negative ... taking risks is part of growing up, but doing so in a way that is prosocial and not a threat to life and limb is desirable.

A need for excitement may also be influenced by the amygdala. The amygdala, Latin for almond due to its shape, is a tiny structure that is also part of the limbic system and plays a number of roles in our behaviour. Generally speaking, the amygdala helps us respond emotionally to a range of experiences and most importantly it is part of our fight-or-flight response system. When out of the blue a dog barks and scares us, it is the amygdala that helps us decide whether to stand our ground or make for the hills! Given its role in our emotional responses at the nexus of an immature brain, the amygdala is one of the of the reasons why adolescents can appear quite moody; they are more likely to overreact to a negative situation instead of responding with the type of controlled response we might see in adults. In simpler terms, the amygdala is responsible for automatic 'hot' responses rather than 'cool' considered responses. Relatedly, the amygdala is also the culprit that plays a role in the propensity for adolescents to misread neutral or inquisitive facial expressions as a sign of anger. In its entirety, it is the amygdala that can lead adolescents to feel that they live in a hostile and dangerous world and their hot response to this world may include various degrees of emotional overreaction and/or aggression ranging from rumour mongering to fisticuffs.

As noted earlier, and taken in its entirety, the myriad of changes in the brain associated with adolescence can be linked to the brain's reward systems and a maturing amygdala. The reward system is partially responsible for changing a child into a restless, exuberant and emotionally intense adolescent desperate to achieve every goal, experience every sensation and fulfil every desire while the amygdala can amplify a vast range of feelings and perceptions. However, while these changes mark an important transition from child to adult as they help to build independence and identity, they can also lead to questionable decisions and a multitude of challenges. Part of the reason for this is not just a product of chemical or maturational changes noted earlier, but can also be found in how an adolescent actually perceives and seeks rewards and views the world.

Concerns around the potentially reckless nature of adolescents often lead adults to think that young people underestimate risks when making decisions. It turns out that that may not necessarily be true. Instead, when making decisions, adolescents tend to overestimate rewards or rather, find rewards more rewarding than any risks associated with those rewards. 'I'll take the carrot and worry about any stick later' is far more prevalent in adolescents as compared to adults. This could be because the nucleus accumbens is much more active in adolescents as compared to children or adults. This is one reason why an adolescent's first love, sporting achievement or other novel experiences can bring on great emotional intensity. Such intensity can be amplified in many ways beyond athletics and friends, including the use of screen devices, which are designed to hook the user by elevating dopamine. This is something to be explored in the next couple of chapters but for now it should be abundantly clear that the adolescent brain is a work in progress.

The information in this chapter is but a snapshot of all the things going on in the developing adolescent brain. A snapshot, but one that projects some of the important considerations related to the types of experiences young people might be engaging in. Moreover, there are enormous challenges associated with educating and guiding such young minds and these challenges are intensified through the interplay of a 21st century, 24/7 media rich world and a brain that took thousands of years to evolve. It is also interesting that older generations often bemoan the plight of the current crop of adolescents, but it could be argued that today's young people actually face cultural and social changes that may not be helping their brain's maturational framework. Increasingly, young people appear to take fewer opportunities to 'do' the types of activities that previous generations experienced and instead spend a great deal of time in a virtual world.

It is important to remember that nature and nurture work in tandem to shape the brain. For example, as the prefrontal lobes of an adolescent mature, they get better at controlling impulses and thinking of others. However, such improvements also require cascades of interactions between individuals and the environment and multitudes of experiences are intimately linked with 'learning'. We learn to make better decisions by making not-so-good decisions and then correcting our behaviour. We become better planners by making plans, implementing them and evaluating the results, again and again. Our social and cultural life is shaped by our biology and vice versa and as such dealing with today's adolescents is not as hopeless as the 'what could they be thinking' catchcry might suggest. It isn't that the adolescent brain's prefrontal lobes just don't show up when they need to, it's just that they need instruction and exercise.

Importantly, such instruction and experience is more powerful and effective when it happens in the real world rather than a virtual one. In fact, there is much to suggest that the virtual world and too much time on screen may actually be defective rather than effective in shaping the minds of young people. The rest of this book expands on that claim, provides evidence to support it and then outlines strategies and ideas for counteracting it.

Entering the Matrix

"I don't like the idea that I'm not in control of my life."

— Neo, *The Matrix*

Fiction Becomes Reality?

In 1999, the hit movie *The Matrix* was seen by millions of viewers worldwide. In hindsight, it was an apt prelude to a new century that was now upon the human race. This science fiction thriller – or dystopian drama, depending on your perspective – showed us a man living two lives. He was Thomas Anderson, a computer programmer by day but by night, he was a computer hacker called Neo. Neo spent much of his time questioning reality while waiting for some kind of sign related to his repeated online encounters with the phrase 'The Matrix'. Little did Neo know, but 'truth' would soon be revealed and he would be transported into a world of binary code known as 'The Matrix'. In this world, Neo would learn that what he knew as reality was actually nothing more that a computer program created by a malevolent Artificial Intelligence. In fact, Neo finds that his reality is actually a façade for sentient machines who grow and harvest people to use as an ongoing energy source.

The complexities of the plot in *The Matrix* are too detailed and expansive to outline here but suffice to say the movie was highly popular and spawned two follow-up films in which Neo continues his adventures in a virtual world. One of the most important messages in this trilogy of films is that everyone has the individual responsibility to make the choice between how much time they spend in the real world of human beings or in an artificial world to be found via technology. Moreover, and with each passing year, that choice is becoming increasingly significant as younger and younger children are spending more and more time on screens and/or online. Relatedly, human beings have a long history of technological advancements, but perhaps none have been as pervasive and omnipotent as that afforded to us via binary code and screen devices. Such a claim requires a detailed history and this chapter is an important look back into how our children have ended up on the verge of existing in their own Matrix.

Our Amazing Minds and Achievements

History is full of amazing human achievements, thanks mostly to the powerful mass of neurons and tissue we call our brain. For thousands of years human beings have used their brains to make life easier. From Stone Age tools, to the wheel, to Gutenberg's printing press and beyond, humankind has excelled at taking nature's raw materials and turning them into whatever made its existence better. In the 20th century our ingenuity started to move us into a world of binary code, microchips and digitisation. Interestingly, young people today are often not aware of how markedly different things were for their parents and grandparents, especially in terms of computers and screen devices. Times have changed very quickly and often with little scrutiny as we take for granted those things that make life easier. In a little over 60 years, we have made exponential changes to our existence by making computers commonplace.

If you were able to travel back in time you would see that it wasn't until the 1950s that computers started to make inroads into modern society. In the early '50s the first computer language COBOL (Common Business-oriented Language) was developed, which was soon followed by FORTRAN (Formula Translation). Try telling a teenager that if you wanted to use a computer you had to be able to do more than swipe a finger across a screen or use a mouse. There was a time when people actually needed to study and learn to speak the language of the device they were using. However, from that time forward, things in the computing world moved quickly until Steve Jobs and Steve Wozniak unveiled the first computer with a single circuit board called the Apple I. Computers were still in their infancy and if you are old enough to remember working on a typewriter, then you will likely remember the day word processing became a reality in 1979.

The '80s were a huge decade, not only for music, 'big' hair and fashion (tongue-in-cheek), but also for introducing the world to 'floppy disks', colour monitors and the first computer to be marketed as a laptop in 1983. Many companies were heavily investing in the rapidly growing world of computer technology, while entrepreneurs and research and design departments were working behind the scenes to make computers a household item and introduce us to the internet and domain names. By the time the '90s had rolled in, many people in western countries were learning to live with, and for, computers, until 1993 when the Pentium microprocessor brought graphics and music to another computer level.

Things really started to advance rapidly before the turn of the century. Microsoft and Apple became the frontrunners in personal devices. Then, just before many began stressing about what would happen when the year 2000 fell upon us with Y2K and the Nostradamus prophecies of planes falling out of the skies due to computers not being able to digitally adapt to a century beginning with the number '2', Wi-Fi appeared and made the World Wide Web that much more accessible. In 2007, the first widely accessible and relatively affordable smartphone was introduced to the world and was followed by an ever-expanding universe of websites, 'apps' (applications), blogs and social media, such as Facebook, Flickr, YouTube, Instagram and Twitter. Humanity was well and truly into the technological thick of it and the stuff of science fiction for previous generations soon become reality for today's! Perhaps this was when we began to enter the Matrix!

We have come a long way since FORTRAN, and the abridged version of events noted above does not even begin to cover the full range of computer and digital ingenuity that has been unleashed on our lives. Of interest to us as researchers, and what should be of interest to you as parents, is to what extent screen technologies have been superfluous or harmful to each digital generation. The millennials of 2000 have now given way to a more screen-absorbed generation and with each passing day young people are online and on screens more than previous generations. Much of this has happened on our watch and been supported by well-meaning parents and teachers, self-promoting schools, political soundbites and tech companies with a profit margin to consider. Mantras of 'one laptop for every child', or 'iPads for all', have become commonplace for anyone seeking to ensure the best life and scholastic outcomes for children. Unfortunately, this has masked some very real issues in terms of educational outcomes and wellbeing. These are two areas that are worthy of elaboration.

Technology and Schooling

Since the advent of the personal computer, education systems have embraced such technologies in schools. From the first desktop computers for students in computer labs, to learning to code, to 'bring your own devices', schools have often embraced technology in the form of accepting computing devices as a must for learners of all ages. What, however, is the current evidence for such claims and what is the current reality in terms of the necessity and utility of computers for learning? We believe these are important considerations, especially given the financial costs of resourcing technology and the dubious claims around the effectiveness and necessity of screen devices.

As noted earlier, computers have revolutionised most aspects of life and work. In the context of education, computers started making inroads into schools and classrooms from the mid-1970s to their seemingly ubiquitous presence across all school sectors in the 21st century. Indeed, it would be very difficult not to find some form of information and computer technologies (ICTs) in the hands and/or classrooms of today's students. It is important to look at the status of such devices given that computers are often held up as a panacea for learning.

When it comes to computers there is often a taken-for-granted notion that they are necessary and an integral component of learning and academic success. Such sentiments are often professed by politicians, ICT specialists, academics and school leaders who use ICTs as marketing tools. As such, they are worthy of careful scrutiny. It is our contention that the growing evidence around screens and device use is worrying and the promotion of such devices as an 'educational must-have' may be complicit in doing more harm than good. However, prior to looking at the potential benefits and/or harms associated with screen devices in schools, it is important to note that identifying them as the specific cause of any particular adverse event or effect is almost impossible. In research terms this is usually articulated as 'correlation does not equal causation'. This is an important consideration when looking at various studies or reports that purport to have hard evidence about anything. At the risk of over-simplification, correlation refers to how some things might be related while causation refers to how something may have directly impacted on something else. It is equally important to note that trying to conduct experiments seeking to identify causation whereby a student or group of students might be harmed through such experience is almost impossible given ethical constraints associated with such research. Therefore, whenever anyone speaks of potential risks associated with screens, for example, we believe that these must be supported by correlation, not causation; harming students to prove a point is not something any good researcher would attempt, or be allowed to attempt. Moreover, just because we are unable to randomly assign students to long-term exposure to screens and then measure the degree of harm to various groups does not mean that there are no established negative effects associated with such activities ... correlation affords us the opportunity to make such claims when supported by corroborative evidence. With that in mind let's look at some of the issues around screen devices in the context of what is often presented as a reality when it may in fact be a myth, or at the very least, 'myth-informed'.

Screen Trends in Schools

The history of various technologies in schools is very diverse and lengthy and as such a more prudent exploration of computers in schools for this chapter originates in the 1980s. During the '80s, there was a steady increase in personal computer use in homes, businesses and schools. I (Michael) was a student during this time and remember the first time I saw a personal computer and heard the hyperbole presented about the future due to advancements in computers and computer technology. As I moved into university, many of my peers were lining up to study the languages of computers as we travelled towards a brave new world. In schools, the culture of positivity around computers was amplified as technology was seen as beneficial for students so that they would be better prepared for the jobs and skills of the future. From such assertions arose a belief that still exists today – that not engaging children in technology will leave them behind. From the outset this seems paradoxical if you think about it. It is likely that most of you have never studied computer programming and yet are quite able to use a computer or smartphone with little difficulty. Two clever social experiments push our skepticism further.

In 1999, researchers from NIIT (a management training company in India), and under the guidance of Dr Sugata Mitra, carved a 'hole in the wall' that separated the NIIT premises from the adjoining slum in Kalkaji, New Delhi.[1] Through this hole, a freely accessible computer was put up for use in what looked like a garden shed. This computer proved to be an instant hit among many of the impoverished that lived in the slum, especially the children. While many adults avoided the computers, the children with no prior experience or instruction learnt to use the computer on their own, through trial and error and fuelled by their curiosity. It is noteworthy that the computers of the time were far less user friendly than those we use today.

Similarly, fast forward to 2012 where another social experiment occurred in Ethiopia under the 'One Laptop Per Child' program which was being implemented in various countries around the globe. 'One Laptop Per Child' was founded by Nicholas Negroponte with a vision to enhance global education by putting a cheap laptop in the hands of some of the most poverty-stricken children on earth. One of the most fascinating outcomes of this philanthropic endeavour occurred in 2012 with 20 Ethiopian children aged six and seven.[2] In an intriguing experiment, representatives from the One Laptop program dropped off closed boxes taped shut and containing small tablets with no instructions to these 20 children.

Many in the organisation, including Nicholas Negroponte, thought that the children would play with the boxes and ignore the devices inside. However, it turned out that within four minutes, one child not only opened the box but also found the on-off switch and powered it up. Within five days, that group of 20 children were using approximately 47 apps per child, per day. And within two weeks, they were singing ABC songs in the village. Their curiosity unabated, it was also reported that within five months, some children had hacked the android operating framework while switching on the camera systems that had been inadvertently disengaged by members of the One Laptop organisation. Like those children in the Indian slums in 1999, and in the absence of any formal instruction, the Ethiopian youngsters demonstrated that their innate curiosity and adventurous spirit was all they needed to get technology working for them.

The preceding two examples are not meant to suggest that there isn't a place for ICTs in schools, but rather are presented to help contest any notion of a child being left behind if they are not provided with computers in schools. Today's technology is designed to be so user friendly that instruction manuals for phones, tablets and computers are either not provided or offer little more than basic start up and warranty information. Moreover, considering the history of rapid advancement and innovation in all measures of ICT, does anyone seriously believe that teaching coding to four-year-old Australian children, as is the case in many schools, will be of any use to them in a decade when they turn 14? This is an important question given the financial resourcing of ICTs and growing evidence that technology, and by association computers and the internet, appear to do little in terms of academic outcomes.

ICTs, Academic Skills and Outcomes

Along with claims suggesting the lack of access to ICTs may hinder a student's technological future, there are also many who position ICTs as integral to notions of improving academic skills and outcomes. Over the past decade many educational innovators have touted technology as a panacea for learning and have been supported by politicians who have placed technology at the forefront of notions of an educational revolution. For example, 15 years ago, then opposition leader Kevin Rudd announced the digital education revolution (DER) program before the 2007 election, which was intended to provide every student in Years 9 to 12 with a laptop. Moreover, this $1 billion dollar initiative would be further funded to purportedly keep laptop use in schools at the cutting edge of technology. Five years after Rudd's announcement, and after a change in leadership, Prime Minister Julia Gillard maintained that pledge whereby the government spent over $2.1 billion on the laptop program. Few would disagree that from such expenditure should come measurable benefits, especially when it comes to educational outcomes, yet any data pertaining to such benefits is not widely available. And while there have been a disparate range of studies across various curriculum and pedagogical areas, well-established research findings in the disciplines of cognitive science, human factors and the psychology of learning suggest that ICTs may in fact have a deleterious impact on learning. For example, the sheer volume of information available to students through the use of computers can create cognitive overload and attentional shifts while the visual nature of devices along with 'pop-ups', instant messages and alerts from 'apps' make devices inherently distracting. Perhaps one could say computers in school create a Matrix of inopportunity for learning.[3] Such concerns are exacerbated by studies and reports related to the use and potential overuse of technology in terms of the very skills and outcomes many technology enthusiasts suggest are enhanced through ICTs in schools. Considering that almost a decade ago researchers found language and learning deficits in 11 to 18-year-old students who used technology excessively,[4] it should not be surprising that questions related to the efficacy and utility of ICTs in schools have grown exponentially and nowhere is this more apparent than in a special report published in 2015 by the Organisation for Economic Co-operation and Development (OECD).[5]

The OECD is familiar to many who work in education and most notably for their international assessments of student performance in reading, mathematical and scientific literacy. Conducted every three years, the Programme for International Student Assessment (PISA) tests 15-year-olds across the three domains noted and publishes those findings with the intent of assisting governments of participating countries to monitor educational outcomes against a common framework. In 2015, 72 countries participated in PISA and the findings indicated that Australia had recorded significant declines in mathematical literacy since 2003, in scientific literacy since 2006 and in reading literacy since 2009. Overall, Australia dropped in its overall rankings and this, in turn, fuelled many political slogans and contentious debates related to those results and what needed to be done. It is important to emphasise that PISA received a great deal of attention and will likely do so after the next iteration of tests takes place. However, and of interest in the context of this chapter, is the silence surrounding the OECD's report on students, computers and learning published in 2015.

Students, Computers and Learning: Making the Connection makes for interesting reading, especially when linked to PISA findings. The report provides an in-depth analysis of ICT usage in OECD countries and the results of this analysis do not present a very positive picture. Consider the following passages from the foreword of the report where Andreas Schleicher, the OECD's Director for Education and Skills notes:

> *… students who use computers very frequently at school do a lot worse in most learning outcomes, even after accounting for social background and student demographics …*

and that

> *… the results also show no appreciable improvements in student achievement in reading, mathematics and science in the countries that had invested heavily in ICT for education …*

and finally,

> ... *put simply, ensuring that every child attains a baseline proficiency in reading and mathematics seems to do more to create equal opportunities in a digital world than can be achieved by expanding or subsidising access to high-tech devices and services.*[6]

Some might suggest that the sentiments above are isolated to one report but interestingly that same report goes on to note that their findings are "remarkably similar to the emerging consensus in the research literature, based on studies that use more rigorously designed evaluations."[7] In other words, the report echoes robust research studies noting that ICTs in school may not be the panacea for learning some would promote as necessary for the future.

The assertions made above do little to support arguments made by ICT enthusiasts regarding the use of screen devices and academic outcomes. Arguably, those enthusiasts might look at the OECD's findings and drive the 'correlation does not indicate causation' barrow noted earlier as a means of negating those findings. Interestingly, and perhaps almost prophetically, the OECD's report notes that the most frequent pattern emerging from the data is a weak and sometimes negative association between investment in ICT usage and learning. Furthermore, as noted earlier, such assertions mirror other empirical studies and evaluations of the efficacy of ICTs in schools.

One such evaluation based on 81 meta-analyses of research published over the past 30 years found that, on average, ICT's effect on learning had little, if any impact as compared to other teaching interventions.[8] If all of this information is an accurate representation of the efficacy of ICTs in schools then the ongoing financial costs of promoting and pushing a device for all children and the continued resourcing of the most recent ICT products does not appear to add any substantive academic benefit. Indeed, the last decade has seen a growing body of research literature concerned with the utility of ICTs in schools. However, any discussion about ICTs in schools needs to go beyond the utility and perceived benefits of devices in classrooms and encompass a broader picture of learning with a particular focus on education's complicity in problems associated with screen devices, mental health and wellbeing.

Screens and Wellbeing

Before looking at examples of the potential impact of screen devices on student wellbeing, it is important to reiterate the proposition that started this chapter in relation to correlation and causation. It is likely that what is about to be presented below will be critiqued by ICT advocates from all backgrounds as correlational. This is a fair comment but unfounded in its overall veracity and accuracy. Remember, we cannot conduct experiments that harm students but that does not mean that studies that speak to potential harms can be discounted. The burden of proof for ICT advocates is to present data indicating the contrary to correlational findings rather than focusing on the nature of studies themselves. Moreover, it is important to consider that educators are bound by the Latin phrase, 'in loco parentis', meaning 'in the place of a parent'. Given the underlying responsibility of that sentiment, teachers, and by association schools, must always bear in mind that they act as parents when at school and as such be willing to consider any evidence related to screen usage and student wellbeing. In other words, blindly accepting computers as a necessity for classroom endeavour without looking at bigger picture issues and challenges is arguably not conducive to any notion of acting like a parent and indeed there is a growing list of studies rendering the rampant use of screen devices as problematic.

The range of issues being researched in relation to screen devices and wellbeing is rather expansive as evident in other chapters in this book, all of which get considerable attention. For this chapter, however, we focus on two areas of concern that schools may be contributing to without even realising they are doing so and then examine some related trends that go beyond the schoolyard. The first of these issues relates to 'distraction' and notions of 'multi-tasking'.

Multi-tasking in its simplest sense may be defined as doing more than one activity simultaneously. Multi-tasking is not a new phenomenon, but technology has arguably reinvigorated research into this area given its capacity for presenting multiple platforms of information simultaneously. One of the most interesting dilemmas with multi-tasking is that when we try to pay attention to more than one thing at a time, such pursuits increase distractibility and slow performance on tasks due to interference in decision making or what is known as 'Cognitive Bottleneck'.[9] In simpler terms, having to switch from one task to another is time-consuming and takes effort and this may be one of the reasons why computers can actually impair performance and distract learners. Concurrently, while many students might suggest that they can easily switch back and forth between tasks, this is arguably nothing more than a reflection of the simplicity of the technology that fails to take into account the negative influence of such activities. There is ample evidence to suggest that students who engage in these types of multi-tasking behaviours dramatically increase the time to complete tasks, the number of memory errors committed and the processing time associated with such activities while simultaneously diminishing any learning requiring complex cognitive activity.[10] Finally, while prolonged multi-tasking may interfere with learning in a myriad of ways, such activity is only symptomatic of broader challenges associated with screen usage that transcend notions of learning and focus more worryingly on wellbeing.

Currently there is a multitude of studies that have explored a range of concerns associated with computer usage, smartphones, video games, social media, the internet and other aspects of technology that we so easily take for granted.[11] Two areas of concern related to wellbeing that schools may be complicit in contributing to are overuse and sleep disturbance. Now you might be thinking that schools do not dictate when a student goes to sleep, but as schools continue to embrace technology it should be self-evident that students will spend more of their waking hours in front of screens. The overuse of technology can be found across a range of studies and the term addiction has now been linked with various aspects of screen devices.[12] Screen and internet addiction are a genuine concern for mental health professionals as evident by an increasing number of reports and studies highlighting the potential consequences of overuse. Furthermore, the *Diagnostic and Statistical Manual* (DSM) of the American Psychiatric Association, the gold standard for diagnosing mental health issues, added internet addiction to its most recent edition.[13] Internet addiction is an emergent disorder and while there exists much debate as to the constituent elements and symptoms of this relatively new mental health issue, anecdotal evidence and reports of parents struggling to separate their children from their screens suggests that we should be mindful of screen time. This is also true of schools that insist on the use of computers during lessons whereby any extra time on screen may be contributing to total daily screen time. Finally and most notably, depending on how much time a student spends on a computer during class time, along with the time they spend on personal devices like smartphones during breaks, there is also reason to worry about a lack of social interaction that is vital for wellbeing.

Humans are social beings! This claim is supported by decades of research telling us that being with other people is a vital component to all measures of development and health. Indeed, if the global pandemic that started in 2019 has taught us anything, it is that isolation via lockdowns makes us unwell. Consider that in the early years of life, all aspects of a child's overall development are impacted by social interaction and the intrinsically human need to engage socially permeates adolescent development and most aspects of healthy adult life. Unfortunately, computers have had a negative impact on this important component of human endeavour. Face-to-face interaction appears to have begun diminishing due to an increase in computers and electronic media use since 1997 and this gap continues to grow as people engage with screens rather than other people.[14] Worryingly, it appears that heavy ICT use at the intersection of social media may also be contributing to feelings of loneliness and anxiety amongst school-aged children.[15] Equally worrisome is the fact that ICTs may be exacerbating various mental health concerns in young people due sleep deprivation.

Not unlike the plethora of research related to the importance of social interaction, there is an equally burgeoning body of research related to numerous aspects of physical and mental health and sleep. This is covered in greater detail in the next chapter but is worthy of foreshadowing here.

It is a well-established scientific fact that sleep is not only important in terms of all aspects of health and healthy development but also in terms of memory, cognition and learning.[16] When we are asleep our brains are busy consolidating memories of recent events and when we are tired due to lack of sleep our capacity for highly functioning cognitive activity is compromised. This has implications for all levels of schooling in that tired minds cannot perform well but it has even greater implications for adolescent students whose sleeping patterns change markedly with the onset of puberty and who appear to be chronically sleep-deprived. Rhetorically speaking, one might ask how schools play a role in the setting sleep times for students and the answer can be found in one word: homework.

Homework, in itself, is a contentious educational phenomenon but the problem with homework may not necessarily be homework per se, but more specifically the guidelines for submitting homework. It is now fairly common practice for schools to provide online submission of assignments coupled with dubious timelines for such submissions – midnight is not an uncommon deadline for handing in assignments! Putting these types of parameters in place sets students up for even greater sleep disturbances in that the light emitted from computers and handheld devices has been shown to suppress the production of melatonin (the neurotransmitter that induces sleep), elevate states of arousal and, by association, negatively impact on sleep patterns and behaviour. Moreover, it is probably a safe assumption that many adolescents leave things to the last minute to complete and may coincidentally be less efficient in completing a task due to notions of multi-tasking discussed earlier, resulting in work being submitted later rather than sooner. Finally, given that adolescents tend to be chronically sleep deprived, it is noteworthy that a recent study of school-aged children in Canada found that losing just one hour of sleep negatively impacted on short-term memory, emotional functioning, attention, working-memory and academic performance. Sleep is essential for children to function productively and get the most out of each day.

It should be evident by now that the glowing light of technology in the lives of children may not be very divine! Screens have made in-roads in schools and indeed contributed much to the collective lives of children and adults alike but we are only beginning to see that all that they provide may not be entirely positive. Could it be that they are metaphorically creating a generation of Neos longing to find their way around the Matrix? And for those who have not seen the film or have forgotten its antagonists, sentient machines known as 'Agents' are set out to destroy Neo and his comrades in an effort to stop humans from escaping the Matrix. Let us hope that we are not too late in awakening you to the Matrix but if so perhaps the next chapter will give you further pause for thought and further determination to help students thrive in the real world rather than getting lost in a virtual one.

The Divine Glow of Screens!

"The two most powerful warriors are patience and time ..."

— Leo Tolstoy

Attention Span, Concentration and the Tricks of Technology

Evolutionary psychologists posit that the human ability to create fire gave rise to more than a convenient heating and cooking source. As we huddled together in our caves, able to transcend the night/day cycle to remain awake and engaged past sundown, we began to find ways to amuse and entertain ourselves when the day's work was done. Indeed that end-of-day reflection, simply sitting and staring into the fire, is legitimately thought to have given rise to one our most extraordinary assets: our imagination.

The human capacity to work with, manipulate, and even invent abstract concepts 'in our heads' is unparalleled by any other species. Starting as early as six months of age, the human baby begins to demonstrate a cognitive ability psychologists refer to as 'object permanence'. Consider what happens after a ball rolls under a couch. An enthusiastic dog may scratch and whine for a while, but eventually will lose interest and wander off when distracted (think squirrel!). Human babies, however, begin to understand that out of sight is not out of mind; they understand that the object they have lost still exists in space and time. Infants have even been shown to stare longer at apparent 'magic' tricks that suggest physical impermanence, suggesting they already understand this is not possible.

Fast forward about 12 years, when that magnificent frontal lobe explodes in sophistication, and all of sudden the understanding that the ball is still under the couch expands into being able to work with abstract concepts, algebra, even complex mathematical proofs – all in our heads. This ability translates to early artworks in caves, the experimentation with different resources to invent solutions to practical problems (pottery, metals), storytelling, singing and dancing, the shared communication and transmission of ideas – all of which no doubt contributed to the continued development of ingenuity. But back to the beginning, might some of this have been facilitated by the time and space to engage in the quiet reflection, meditation and processing of new information as our ancestors sat and stared quietly into the fire?

Much more is now known about modern human attention capacity, its strengths, weaknesses and limitations. Many have probably heard of the seven plus or minus two capacity of our working memory. Simply put, most people can juggle between five and nine items in their head (think shopping lists, phone numbers etc.) before they become overwhelmed. What is less known is that all our attentional faculties have limits – there are simply only so many things we can process at once. For example, in the famous Invisible Gorilla Experiment, people are presented with two teams of three or four individuals. One team is wearing white t-shirts while the other is dressed in black. While watching the teams, the participants are asked to count the number of ball passes made by one of the selected teams as they move around and pass the ball among their similarly clad team members. Not long after the experiment starts, another actor dressed in a gorilla suit then walks into the middle of the group, does a brief dance, and wanders off screen. This is where it gets interesting. After the teams stop passing the ball, the observers are asked to reveal how many passes were made. If they get the number of passes correct they rarely, if at all, notice the gorilla unless previously told or cued to do so. They are so focused on completing the task of counting passes, they miss the glaringly obvious human masquerading as one of our primate cousins. As unbelievable as this sounds, it unfolds this way every time, and reminds us that there's only so much we can focus on at once. Our attentional focus has limits, and if we've been given a task to do, we can easily overlook a distraction if it is unrelated to that task.

Aside from a growing understanding of the limitations of attention, we also know that it can be manipulated. It's no coincidence that some of our most highly-paid psychiatrists and psychologists are employed by marketing companies and advertisers. Their job is to ensure they can attract and maintain customers' attention long enough for them to form a positive impression of whatever product they are trying to flog. Bonus points if they can convince them that they truly *need* a product that they almost certainly do not.

For those professionals who seek to gain and maintain your attention, the advent of the ubiquitous screen in your pocket has created a new focal point that can be commandeered by marketers to their full benefit. Their job is to ensure you leap to attention and check your phone the second you hear that 'ding'! Sound familiar? The easiest way to do this is to invoke the same training technique used by gambling games – most especially pokies – known as 'irregular intermittent reinforcement'. Put simply, you will receive a reward for answering your phone on occasion, but it will be seemingly at random. This particular way of delivering rewards excites you and lights up your anticipatory dopamine systems.

If you recall from Chapter 2, dopamine is a neurotransmitter or chemical messenger in the brain that creates feelings of pleasure and reward, which can drive you to repeat specific behaviours. Of interest here, and alluded to earlier, is that the unpredictability of receiving a reward increases anticipation and dopamine release or what is known as 'anticipatory' dopamine. Why is anticipatory dopamine so important? Consider the buzz you get when you smell bread breaking, or the crackling atmosphere in the stadium before a game begins, or how the heart flutters before your crush walks into a room. The experience of anticipation is almost always more exciting than finally engaging in the real thing. Let's face it … coffee never tastes as good as it smells.

Anticipatory dopamine is an incredibly powerful force as it drives us to 'do something' in order to access our reward. Even if we are disappointed time after time, all of a sudden, when we least expect it, bingo! We receive our prize. So we leap to attention to answer the 'ding' because even though it's more likely to be our mum, friend, or work colleague contacting us – what if it's that gorgeous person we're hoping to date, or an exciting job offer we've been waiting on? The anticipation drives us to answer. The same methods, with the help of technology, are used to tune us into the news, updates, information – most of the time it's mind-numbingly boring nonsense, but every now and then it's extraordinary and important news.

These techniques are deliberately used to manipulate people into responding time and time again to the 'ding' that usually heralds nothing more than pointless and useless information, in the faint hope that just for once something interesting pops up on our screen. One real problem is: what is that constant beck and call, scrolling and searching for something remotely interesting, taking us away from?

Australian cartoonist Michael Leunig found himself at the mercy of various social apologists and accused of misogyny in 2019 when he dared to draw a cartoon depicting the truth of phone addiction for far too many parents and children. His cartoon showed a mother so intent on her phone while wheeling the pram, that she hadn't noticed her baby had fallen out of it, and kept on walking, all the while intent on her phone.

Rather than inspire some self-reflection and community discussion about the misuse of technology and its broader impact in society, the personal abuse hurled at Leunig for daring to point out an ugly societal truth was well and truly in line with what happens to anyone who tries to take a substance away from an addict.

Even more ironically, his cartoon appeared shortly after a series of news reports from lifeguards and managers of council pools noting an increase in the rise of near-deaths and actual fatalities from children drowning while their parents sat by, glued to their phones.[1] Some of these children died while their parents sat by the pool. The lack of perspective among hand-wringers supporting parents' 'right' to relax and enjoy uninterrupted 'me-time' was jaw-dropping. We would be remiss if we failed to point out that this is not just happening in Australia. Type into Google 'drownings, parents on phone' to see an international sweep of just how widespread this problem has become.

Individuals, young and old, are becoming increasingly addicted to, and dependent on, their smartphones for constant entertainment, distraction and attention. This is a more significant issue for younger people; as any drug-dealer or tobacco company executive knows, the earlier the dependency is formed, the harder it is to break later on in life.

The constant dinging and delivery of information titbits is also driving down a young person's capacity to concentrate for long periods of time. For a start, any task requiring focused concentration would mean they would need to hide their smartphone from themselves for several hours to undertake such a task! Relatedly, the inability to become engrossed in a novel, or work their way through complicated hypotheses, ideas and philosophies in the context of a series of constant interruptions is resembling a form of artificial ADHD (attention deficit hyperactivity disorder). In other words, their brains are potentially being wired towards favouring decreasing 'bits' of information over long, complex thought processes.

So what might be the knock on effects of our new ways of engaging with the highway of information coming our way? We receive endless 'tweets', 'notifications' and 'headlines': tiny bits of information that act as clickbait but do little to inform us at any deep level. Their job is to make people react, and in that they are alarmingly successful. How many people genuinely go behind the headline news to critically contemplate the information dispensed, and weigh up the source, their agenda, or even the logical consistency (or lack thereof) of the ideas being presented?

Headlines, Outrage and the Dumbing Down of Debate

Master manipulators have realised just how powerful a well-targeted message can be. Protests, even riots, can be easily triggered by a carefully crafted missile into a shallow attention span longing for a reason to react.

And remember Theory of Mind from Chapter 2? This very skill that is a significant deficiency in autism, appears to be diminishing in younger cohorts, hence the title of this book. If you cannot make time to contemplate, process and critically think about another person's perspective, what is that doing to your Theory of Mind? Rather than genuinely engaging in robust debates about conflicting ideas, society is quickly devolving into a constant game of 'playing the man instead of the ball'. Or, in other words, shooting the messenger instead of debating the intellectual content of the message! A fascinating example can be seen in the experiences of the legendary tennis player and ironically LBG trailblazer Martina Navratilova.

In 2019, Navratilova expressed her alarm at the rising number of transgender women dominating the female sides of what has been, until recently sex-segregated competitions. The science around this topic is becoming increasingly uncontroversial. If a human body has gone through an androgenising puberty, as males do, there are clear physical benefits in the sporting arena (e.g. increased bone density, muscle strength and VO2 max to name but a few). Navratilova's contention was that in elite sports this is unfair. A 1% difference in ability means the difference between a Gold and Bronze medal, therefore consider the advantage – 10%, 20%, 30% or more – conferred by a chromosome swap (X to Y) and its downstream consequences on biological development. In other words, a biological male has distinct advantages regardless of subjective self-identification as being transgender.

Having said that, our point actually isn't about what side of the debate you sit on regarding transgender representation in elite sports – each side has interesting arguments to put forth. What we would like to highlight was how Navratilova's concerns played out. Instead of inviting trans-expert endocrinologists, sports scientists or specialists to comment on her concerns, Navratilova was viciously trolled as a TERF (trans-exclusionary radical feminist) and faced a storm of increasingly personal slanders. Rather than debating her concerns, the focus never shifted from attempting to silence or 'cancel' her comments. She was dropped from advisory bodies and faced a barrage of online abuse. Ask yourself: what is the purpose of this behaviour? How does this in any way lead to constructive debate or deepen each side's understanding of the complexities of this topic?

In amongst this firestorm, World Ruby Union quietly banned male-to-female transgender athletes from competing in female rugby teams given the nature of their full body contact sport, which comes with inherent injury risk. Citing the rising tide of evidence, a sport already grappling with issues around concussion simply couldn't put female athletes at further risk by allowing persons with a biologically impossible-to-match strength advantage into their midst.

In questioning the background agenda to this current situation, ask yourself why sex segregation in sports was introduced in the first place. Then query why sex was swapped with gender. When or how did this happen and what was the rationale? Good luck finding those answers, because whenever this topic rears its head, it's immediately met with hysteria, outrage and cry-bullies demanding a cancellation. It has become impossible to ask a legitimate question without censure.

We have provided this topical debate as but one example for the purpose of illustrating the importance of analytical thought and 'Theory of Mind'. We're sure readers are right now thinking about a smorgasbord of other taboo topics where they'd genuinely appreciate more intelligent and constructive information. Consider now the dual impact of poor attention, and poor Theory of Mind, in attempting to engage in these complex topics of community concern. We are seeing a perfect storm of clickbait headlines that seek to polarise readers along their already-held belief systems, followed by a torrent of abuse for the person daring to ask a difficult question, followed by an inability to process complex information or move outside the reader's original perspective. This inevitably leads to digging in of one's heels, as opposed to an opening up of one's mind ...

We will be expanding on these issues in our social media chapter. For now, we'd like to quickly outline some more fundamental problems associated with increasing screen time.

What Else Could You Be Doing?

If you're glued to your phone, what are you not doing instead? First, screens rob people of exercise and physical activity. The benefits of physical activity are surely a no-brainer to most readers. By way of displacement, our increasing screen time is leading to increasing sedentary time. So much so that sitting has been described as the 'new smoking'. The physical problems here are so well known, we've decided not to waste readers' time and move on instead to thinking about the psychosocial impacts.

Parents are often told they need to get their kids outside to play to combat childhood obesity – which is more widespread than ever. But too much screen time does more than just make our kids fat. We know that spending prolonged periods in front of screens isn't only bad for weight management in kids, it has also been shown to be detrimental to cognitive development, psychological health and sleep.[2]

From a psychological perspective, children get a kick out of feeling effective and in control of themselves in their surroundings. Remember the look of glee on your child's face when they took their first steps, mastered a puzzle, first kicked a footy? Furthermore, most people also prefer to choose activities that appeal to them. These two crucial factors in building psychological wellbeing are referred to by psychologists as 'competence' and 'autonomy'. Providing play opportunities that increase physical activity, alongside promoting both competence and autonomy, will result in genuine skill development, as well as creating an enhanced sense of self-efficacy and psychological wellbeing.

So following are some questions and possible solutions. Let's start by thinking about what are the addictive properties deliberately developed to hook your child (and even yourself) into increasing dependence on that screen in your pocket. How is a screen device genuinely useful to you? How is it genuinely harmful?

Some good habits to cultivate for both parents and children include that age-old wisdom of moderation, combined with a little modern mindfulness. When you find yourself reaching for your phone without any prompts to do so, ask yourself the following:

> What am I doing?
>
> Why am I doing this?
>
> Could I be doing something more useful with my time?
>
> What are the impacts of this behaviour?
>
> Is this behaviour consistent with my long-term goals?

Now if you are searching for important information, scheduling work, or are genuinely in need of a bit of downtime, fair enough. However, be honest with yourself when you are really just wasting time, looking for a distraction, or procrastinating, ignoring a task you know you should be doing instead!

Aside from actively considering your motivations for grabbing a phone, make certain there are times and places designated as screen free zones. The dinner table is a great place to start. Some restaurant groups now insist on all phones being placed in the middle of the dining table and the first person to crack and reach for that 'ding' has to buy a round of drinks!

And what about your daily routines and learned habits? Are you grabbing your phone first thing in the morning? Or last thing at night? Consider what your daily screen habits have displaced – conversation or affection from your partner, getting up and moving about, chores/recreation? What about sleep? Sleep in adolescence is particularly important, and a plethora of research points to screens, especially hand held devices in the bedroom, having negative effects on sleep with knock-on impacts to mood and cognitive function throughout the following day; remember the discussion of sleep in Chapter 2. Is it any wonder that our new generation of partnered young adults is now having less sex than their forefathers? That's right millennials, your boomer parents were more horizontally active than you!

Finally, reflect upon the more complex tasks your brain can undertake given the opportunity. Of course it's easier to sit back and be a passive recipient of entertainment, and there's absolutely nothing wrong with giving your brain a rest at the end of a hard day. But when did you really 'think' about a topic? It doesn't have to be some social issue de jour, maybe you need to consider what you're doing in your career, your relationship, as a parent, with your health. When did you earnestly devote some real thinking time to process, work through, gather information and develop a better understanding of your situation and your future goals? Use that magnificent organ to its full capacity, instead of keeping it amused with pointless titbits. Concentrate, try to see something from another's perspective – we are all better people for cultivating these abilities.

Another seriously important consideration is that of parents modelling responsible screen use behaviours to their children, so they understand from day one that there is a time and place for screens, and a time and place to fully engage in reality. Now we appreciate this is easier said than done. One of us (Rachael) had the joy of managing a toddler during the pandemic and is happy to admit an over-reliance on screens during lockdown. However, a rather horrifying trend started to appear. Said toddler started to have massive tantrums when the screen was removed, and it came as no surprise that a lot of the sites he was visiting employed exactly the same nefarious techniques of intermittent reinforcement, only this time hidden within kids' videos.

Ultimately the cold turkey approach was employed – when the lockdown lifted, the toddler was informed his tablet had broken (parental code for 'it is actually hidden upstairs in the wardrobe'). About 72 hours of whinging and occasional tantrums ensued until the impact started to weaken. It was a couple of weeks before he really got back to normal playing outside and with his toys. But here's the thing, managing a three-year-old tantrum is a vastly different undertaking from wrangling with a strong six-foot male 15-year-old's beastly meltdown.

Relatedly, what we are seeing far too often are parents who have allowed this addiction/distraction to drift on for too long. They wheel in their 15-year-old, totally addicted to the latest video game, refusing to come out of their room, or to go to school, or engage in any social activity. Perhaps it's not too late to help this screenager and his exasperated parents, but it's exceedingly more difficult to remedy. For mental health professionals and educators, desperate parents will often present this altered human asking them to 'fix their kid'. Please have another read of Chapter 1 and remind yourself that the human brain wires itself to the environment in which it finds itself. If your child's brain has been allowed to fester in a world of online unreality with all the deliberate tricks of addiction used to keep it there – what skills and abilities have they now? And what skills and abilities have they displaced?

By ensuring the opportunity to disengage from this constant distraction, which invites shallow attention formation, you will be offering them the opportunity to think, to dream, to process and reason with difficult concepts. Just like our ancestors before us, having some time and patience to contemplate allows our clever brains to work to their potential, and remains vital to the development of understanding, imagination and ingenuity.

The Usual Suspects: Violence, Addiction, Cyberbullying and Cybersex

"For the first time in history, children are growing up whose earliest sexual imprinting derives not from a living human being, or fantasies of their own ... the sexuality of children has begun to be shaped in response to cues that are no longer human. Nothing comparable has ever happened in the history of our species ... they are being imprinted with a sexuality that is mass-produced, deliberately dehumanizing and inhuman."

— Naomi Wolf, *The Beauty Myth*

Today's children live in a 24/7 media rich interconnected reality of virtual activity. The Australian Bureau of Statistics[1] reported that for the period of 2016-2017, 97% of households with children under 15 years had access to the internet, with an average number of 7.8 devices per home. 99% of households with children under 15 years used a mobile or smartphone to access the internet, and social media was rapidly becoming the preferred news source among young people. But what, precisely, are children being exposed to via these conduits? Of course there are many positives. Gone are the days when heated family arguments erupted over "What's the name of that actor?" or "What's the capital of Uzbekistan?" Our devices bring with them a highway of information coupled with convenience of access.

Unfortunately, such conveniences do not come without challenges and concerns. The dark side of this tsunami of data can be summed up in two broad categories: violence and sex. And, quite often, an interaction between the two. Some might think that violence and sex have been around for a long time and older generations had their fair share of watching violent or pornographic movies, for example. However, ease of access has created a very different world for young people and by association is shaping their brains, minds and behaviour in ways we are only beginning to understand. So what is the effect of these exposures on a growing brain?

Violence and the Developing Brain

For many years people have wondered about the influence of various forms of violent media on child development. When the television first entered people's homes in the late 1940s, very few could afford them but by the early 1950s those numbers began to grow exponentially. When Neil Armstrong stepped onto the moon in 1969, millions sat glued to the TV screen to see this achievement. It wasn't too much longer before television began to broadcast for the sake of entertainment and titillation rather than news and education. Soon after, developmental psychologists began to scrutinise what impact TV was having on children, particularly if they were witnessing any forms of violence. Even the animated actions of Bugs Bunny and other popular cartoon characters became cause for concern. After all, what was stopping a child from copying Wile E. Coyote's incessant desire to harm the Roadrunner and drop an anvil on an unsuspecting sibling? Even today, and within the parameters of Social Learning Theory,[2] the mantra of 'children see, children do' is used to push certain agendas and keep parents hypervigilant about their own behaviour in front of their kids. With the recent advances in technology since the turn of the century, concerns over what is consumed via television screens is exacerbated by the reality that children can now watch most things, anytime, in the palm of their hand. For example, while the use of screens, and in particular social media, to stream extreme violence is a relatively new issue, researchers have struggled to keep up with potential impacts of streamed acts of actual violence in real-time on the developing brain.

There are some things we are just starting to understand. Exposure to violence can lead to desensitisation, which can contribute to later acts of violence in adolescence. Peer norms are also important here in that teens will tend to mimic the mood or context in which it is shared (horror and disgust versus amusement and sarcasm). It is probably fair to speculate that peers sharing violent content for a laugh could provide a perfect storm of desensitisation and tacit peer approval for acts of extreme violence.

The impact of streaming violent imagery on children varies depending on age. Younger kids may struggle to understand that another person holds a different, yet valid, perspective to their own (Theory of Mind). Children may assume the threat presented in violent media is immediate and likely to affect them. They will also struggle to put rare versus common events into perspective because of their limited abstract reasoning. Teenagers are still at risk of personalising and catastrophising the risk towards them and their peers in general, but are less likely to react with fear and anxiety compared to their younger counterparts.

In all, we have good reason to believe that continued exposure to violent acts streamed via social media can lead to desensitisation, with knock-on effects of lowered empathy and heightened fear and anxiety. A fearful person with lowered empathy is at greater risk of committing future aggressive and/or violent acts themselves in times of perceived threat – worth bearing in mind before believing teens become immune to the constant bombardment of this imagery.

Screens and Social Media Addiction

Remember the section in the preceding chapter about intermittent reinforcement schedules and how smart devices are set up to employ every trick in the book to get people hooked? What we didn't cover was the results of increasing screen time and social media addiction ... they shouldn't really be a surprise to anyone who has ever spent time with any kind of addict.

Being addicted to something can lead to a vast array of personal and social issues. And while most people have heard of, or know of someone, who may have dealt with more familiar addictions, such as alcohol and/or drugs, there are others that may not be as widely known. For example, addiction to various aspects of screen devices is an increasing area of concern for those who work in the fields of child and adolescent development and psychology. Indeed, internet addiction and in particular addiction to gaming is now listed in the American Psychiatric Association's *Diagnostic and Statistical Manual of Mental Disorders (DSM-5)*.[3] This expansive volume of work is the 'bible' for diagnosing mental health disorders and used by mental health professionals across the globe. Unfortunately, the relative newness of screen devices has not provided us with as much data as we'd like but a growing number of studies suggest that screen-related addictions are certainly worthy of concern. This is especially true when we consider that more time on social media has been associated with higher anxiety and being diagnosed with an anxiety disorder,[4] while internet addiction has been linked with higher levels of rumination, low self-care, social problems and poor academic performance.[5]

The depth of concern related to children and adolescents and social media extends beyond Australia's borders and is evident in extensive data samplings of American teens. Studies looking at changes across generations have found that the psychological wellbeing of American adolescents has dramatically decreased over the last 40 years, and this appears to be directly linked to time spent on electronic communication and screens, including social media, and spending less time participating in non-screen activities (sport, homework, in-person interaction).[6,7]

Complementary research has found that students who visited internet sites focussed on visual depiction (Instagram, Snapchat) for more than two hours per day, reported higher body image concerns and mental health concerns compared to those who did not.[8] In short, the social media space is giving adolescents a warped perception of the world and the people in it. Fear of missing out (FOMO) and feeling inadequate against a backdrop of perfect lives/bodies is creating a sense of frustration that one simply can't 'measure up'. The fakeness of these Facebook/Instagram avatars is still lost on many teens, as they are more likely to believe at face value the imagery that's being served to them. As one of our psychology students once quipped, "I'm not only jealous of other people's Facebook pages; I'm jealous of my own! Because in reality, that's not my life ..."

Cyberbullying

Most would agree that very few kids will get through life without encountering bullying. We all remember the schoolyard taunts, the stealing/destruction of property, even the occasional pulling of hair, hitting and punching. However, yesterday's taunts or punch in the nose have been replaced with arguably more nefarious and psychologically damaging attacks. The major difference between then and now, that has been pointed out ad nauseum by many social scientists, is that once upon a time, the bullying ended at the school gate. Children could at least retreat to home, work, the local playground and physically distance themselves from the bully. This ability to escape provided them with at least some space to process the events of the day or perhaps even an opportunity to talk to someone, strategise and come up with some solutions to the bullying.

But what now? Today's bully can follow a person home, in the car, to work, even into their bedroom at night, ever-present via the smartphone in the back pocket. Bullying is becoming more insidious too, and there is no reprieve for the victim. Research into sex differences in bullying provide further insights into how the traditional schoolyard thug is being replaced by the nasty little internet troll.

In one experiment,[9] preschool boys and girls were given one valued toy to share between them. The boys tended to be very direct in their attempts to obtain the toy, either asking for it or snatching it. And I think we all know that, if not mediated by an adult, snatching can very quickly turn into a slap, hit or punch. Girls, on the other hand, tended to be more passive-aggressive and instead bullied by exclusion i.e. ignoring the girl with the wanted toy and playing their own game. Eventually the girl with the toy gave it up in order to be included in the group.

The researchers noted that in an online context, bullying by exclusion or the spreading of malicious rumours (perhaps with doctored photos and the like) is on the rise among both sexes but more prevalent in females. In other words, the modern bully is adapting their tactics to the new digital playground. Bullying by exclusion still appears to more dramatically impact females, with teenage girls far more vulnerable to its effects. Suicide in younger girls is becoming more prominent with practitioners pointing an accusatory finger at social media as the background culprit. At a recent conference we attended, a leading paediatrician commented that seeing a suicidal nine-year-old used to be a rare and shocking event, but nowadays she was no longer "even surprised." Indeed, in its submission to the Human Rights Commission regarding suicidal behaviour in children, the Child and Youth Mental Health Service (CYMHS) noted that thwarted belongingness (unmet desire for connection with others) was one of the more dangerous precursors to suicidal ideation.[10]

Cybersex

This almost needs no introduction but, to set the scene as it were, pornography is readily available on the internet with one source describing 12% of all websites as pornographic and 25% of all searches being for porn.[11] It also appears that roughly one quarter of adolescents have unintentionally been exposed to online pornography and many of the unintended viewers are distressed by the exposure.[12]

While there are a myriad of issues associated with pornography, one that is understood by most, is that sex in pornography is depicted as wholly disconnected from a caring relationship, instead presenting a variety of largely impossible poses; positions that are best for camera angles, and not for human anatomy! Such depictions essentially teach adolescents how to 'do it like they do on the Discovery channel' which then leads to unrealistic expectations and beliefs about sexual encounters and sexual intimacy.

By way of example, the excellent documentary film *Love and Sex in an Age of Pornography*[13] included interviews with several teenagers about their sexual development in the context of digital porn exposure; many of whom described near-unbelievable sexual encounters that had been influenced by porn. One male teen described losing his virginity:

First time I had sex, cause I'd watched so much porn ... I thought all chicks dig this, all chicks want this done to them, all chicks want it up here, all chicks love it there. I tried all this stuff and yeah ... it went ... bad ...

For most adults this level of inability to separate fantasy from reality seems incredulous, but remember that the adolescent brain does not function like that of an adult. A sophisticated Theory of Mind is still developing and, as the opening quote of this chapter reminds us, what are adolescents learning from?

Let's go back to some brain basics. The average age of first exposure to pornography is 11 years, and at this age the mind of a child is genuinely unable to separate reality from fantasy. This is why younger kids often become scared in films and why an M rating is set at 15 years. Now we throw in some 'classical conditioning'. The young adolescent and their genitals become aroused by unrealistic, often violent and degrading images of sexual contact, separated from any kind of relational interaction. The bodies are all airbrushed and perfect. Fun fact: labiaplasty, unheard of in previous generations, is one of the fastest-growing cosmetic procedures! Even nipple-resizing is now all the go. And we think most readers already know the average male penis is not nine inches erect – an apparently standard requirement for male porn actors! So the young adolescent brain becomes 'wired' for an attraction towards impossible bodies, with even more impossibly proportioned genitalia. Males are visually aroused, and generally, the more voracious users of porn and are particularly vulnerable to developing a slew of strange ideas as to what sex should look like.

On top of their ideas, a new anatomical phenomenon has occurred in boys, known as 'death grip'. The adolescent male masturbates to the imagery they see in pornography, essentially desensitizing their penis over time. When they finally have the opportunity to encounter a real body, the mouth or vagina of that person doesn't even register as noticeable sensation for the male. About the only 'cure' for death grip is a total porn/masturbation ban, so the male brain and penis can recalibrate to an actual human being.

Aside from being desensitised to the real world by watching a virtual one, nearly 100% of 15-year-old males and 80% of 15-year-old females report that they have been exposed to violent, degrading online pornography, usually before they have had a sexual experience themselves. Nearly 90% of the scenes viewed included acts of physical aggression and nearly half verbal aggression.[14] Relatedly, porn misrepresents pleasure, as the actors frequently pretend they are enjoying uncomfortable, painful or humiliating sexual acts. For example, it is well known that over 90% of females require clitoral stimulation to achieve sexual pleasure and/or orgasm, yet a recent British survey demonstrated nearly one third of males could not accurately locate or label this rather vital part of sexual anatomy in females![15]

Go back to the example we gave at the beginning of this section of the teenage male who thought his first-time sexual partner would just love it if he roughly shoved everything into every orifice, and suddenly this makes sense. Porn renders adolescent males with an inability to engage in authentic intimacy by providing them with continued virtual fallacies.

What of the girls in all of this? Another fascinating study took a look at certain pornographic trends that are inherently painful and unlikely to cause pleasure. Unless you've been off the grid and in the woods for the last ten years, you've probably seen or heard about the rise and rise of anal sex depictions in pornography. Interestingly, males have a prostate gland that can be stimulated internally via the anus, so there is an anatomical reason why some men might enjoy this sexual practice. However females have no such gland and therefore the anatomical benefits to women engaging in anal sex are somewhat questionable. A British study[16] concluded that young people have now normalised coercive and painful anal sex, with the young people themselves mainly reporting they wanted to copy what they saw in porn. A submission to the 2019 House of Representatives Standing Committee on Social Policy and Legal Affairs 'Inquiry on age verification for online wagering and online pornography' included an anecdote from a GP who had been seeing increased internal injuries caused by frequent anal sex. She noted:

> *I'm afraid things are much worse than people suspect ... these girls are very young and slight and their bodies are simply not designed for that." They had lied to their mums about it and felt they couldn't confide in anyone else, which only added to their distress ... they said they were humiliated by the experience but they had simply not felt they could say no. Anal sex was standard among teenagers now, even though the girls knew it hurt.*[17]

We need to stress that we are not trying to 'kink-shame' anyone here. Whatever floats your boat! The issue is how do teenagers once again differentiate between fantasy and reality? How do young adults ensure they are communicating honestly and effectively their likes/dislikes and respectfully negotiate sexual boundaries? And what happens when those likes have been shaped and heavily reinforced by pornography rather than experience, with little regard for anatomical realties?

Expectations of females are rather challenging when it comes to intimacy in the 21st century. The pressure on young women to look a certain way, possess 'perfect' genitals, and engage in sex acts that are inherently painful/uncomfortable with partners who have little clue as to the pleasure centres of their anatomy, is testing the mettle of this generation. Imagine being in a so-called loving relationship with someone who is keen to hurt you during sexual contact? Yet this is what is normalised time and time again through pornography. It's no wonder teenagers/young adults are finding sex less and less interesting, with the current younger generation having less frequent sex than their baby boomer grandparents.

It is always important, when talking of issues related to children, adolescents and the virtual world to remember that the human brain does not mature until the mid to late 20s. This means that the immature mind is constantly being shaped and influenced by the stimulation the brain takes in every moment. As such, one final concern regarding the pornography-wired brain is that it fails to develop a sense of sexuality that is respectful, mutual and consenting. Because of this, we now find ourselves in a 'consent crisis', which is entirely predictable as social skills diminish or are hampered in the unrealistic virtual world of pornography. A later chapter will cover in more detail how we develop social skills and, more importantly, how our Theory of Mind can become more sophisticated in picking up nuances of non-verbal expressions, tone and emotion-recognition. For now, we think you will understand what we will be outlining in that chapter is a severe decline in these skills across the generations as a direct consequence of time spent online.

As noted earlier, the content of online porn actually misrepresents much of human intimacy. Where does this leave relationship-building, and sexual relating? How do you 'know' a girl is flirting with you? How do you 'know' a boy really likes you but is too afraid of rejection to ask you out? How do you 'know' a person is initiating sexual contact, wants to continue with it, is enjoying it? Seriously reflect on these questions – how *do* you know?

The #MeToo movement has brought to prominence the difficulties that can arise when people get their wires crossed. Now we in no way wish to diminish the very clear and obvious acts of sexual violence and harassment that many women have faced, and continue to face in their workplaces, or indeed any places they inhabit. However, a number of these transgressions have left a few people scratching their heads. One of the most famous examples was the allegation levelled against Aziz Ansari – which polarised readers and raised a series of fascinating questions as to where responsibility lies in the case of an unsatisfactory sexual encounter.

Ansari took a date home, and they began to engage in sexual contact. The date felt that Anzari was ignoring her signs of discomfort and that she felt compelled to go further sexually than she was comfortable with. Unfortunately, she didn't directly voice these concerns, and in fact when she finally did so, Ansari made no scene nor put up any objections and she left. What followed was an account of their encounter that had readers identifying with either side (Ansari or his date) and every shade of grey in between. What was interesting though, was the date's expectation that Ansari should have 'known' the discomfort she was feeling.

Sadly we are hearing accounts similar to Anzari's date time and time again, with girls assuming boys have the same level of Theory of Mind as they do (they really don't) and that their discomfort should be obvious (how so?). Relatedly we are seeing girls who lack the confidence to negotiate boundaries around sexual interactions for fear of appearing inadequate or upsetting their male partner. This is a lose-lose situation.

We will delve further into the stunted development in communication, non-verbal expression recognition and other communication skills in an upcoming chapter. But perhaps reflect at this point on how intimacy-building and respectful mutual relationships are likely to be hampered by even minor impairments in these fundamental human skills of relating to one another. And as we contend, online pornography does not make for a very good life coach when it comes to relationships and intimacy. Nor does social media in general, which is the fodder for conversation in the next chapter.

Social Media or Social Disease – The Girls Are Not All Right

"Because you are women, people will force their thinking on you, their boundaries on you. They will tell you how to dress, how to behave, who you can meet and where you can go. Don't live in the shadows of people's judgement. Make your own choices in the light of your own wisdom."

— Amitabh Bachchan

Social Comparison and Exclusion

The 21st century certainly has brought with it some challenges not seen – at least in this magnitude – before the onslaught of social media. If you cast your mind back to Chapter 5 where we looked at cyberbullying, and the particular vulnerability of girls, we can take that information and link it to some new psychological phenomena that are proving especially damaging to females. If you recall, girls, teenage girls and younger women are particularly sensitive to social exclusion. So much so, 'bullying by exclusion' is a bona fide new term in human resources circles. The angst that accompanies being left out, excluded and rejected is certainly nothing new, but once again the extraordinary platform provided by social media to toss out an 'undesirable' individual has heightened the experiences of those not part of the cool crowd. This does not make a girl feel good at all.

A number of psychiatrists, psychologists and youth mental health experts are now pointing a collective finger towards social media in explaining the rise and rise of anxiety among teens (especially girls) and the increasingly lower age at which children present with suicidal ideation. You only need to type 'social media and suicide' into Google Scholar to find an alarming number of peer-reviewed articles alongside compelling overviews from frontline physicians dealing with the end point for anxious, rejected and bullied teens. So what is going on here? A few psychological concepts may help us to understand. We can start by looking at 'social comparison'.

Social comparison is a self-explanatory term. Imagine being the prettiest girl in the village a century or two ago. How many females of your age could you compare yourself against? Ten, maybe 100? By way of example, the protagonist of the famous book and movie *Gone With the Wind*, Scarlett O'Hara, comes to mind, for she was famed for having the smallest waist across three counties. Set in the 1860s in the American South, against how many others might Scarlett have been able to compare herself to for the title of smallest waist?

Fast-forward to today, and jump online to scroll through the 'Instathins' and 'Fakebook' posts where girls of all ages show and compare their body sizes. When poring over these images, girls are likely to be comparing themselves against the 0.001% who represent the current cultural ideal.

The genetic outliers that embody current cultural ideals bear no resemblance to the average person. Add in a raft of photoshopping, filters and professional photography and, quite frankly, final Insta-images probably bear little resemblance to the Instagrammer themselves! Unfortunately, teens aren't critical or cynical while they are cast adrift in this sea of impossible beauty standards and never-ending perfection. Remember, their frontal lobes haven't quite developed, and they are still rather emotional. They are also, by nature, peer-focussed and peer-obsessed. Social comparison is how they learn where they fit in society – and so it has always been.

So how might adolescent and young adult females feel if they are using social media as their comparison base? How do they feel when they scroll through images of impossibly idealised women? How do they feel when they find out their boyfriend 'follows' a number of these avatars? How do they feel when they find out their partner would rather masturbate to these images than have real sex with them? How do they feel when no amount of dieting and bodysculpting (or labiaplasty) will get them even close to one of these images? We contend that such sentiments might make a girl feel rather unimportant, redundant, or at the very least, inadequate. What's worse, movements such as body positivity or other confidence-building attempts are largely pointless when society continually reinforces the message that a particular image is key.

Research we were recently part of looked at the impact of the 'like' button on Facebook and found some key negative impacts on young women especially. A confounding question for us is how does a girl navigate the stated message that your outward appearance is less important than your inward self when she will receive thousands of 'likes' for a bikini pic, compared to a few dozen for a photo in her graduation gown? Society via social media has brought out the worst in shallow appearance-based evaluations, and it is relentless and contagious.

Social Contagion

Social contagion is a fancy way of explaining how people begin to copy or mimic the behaviours of those closest to them – or in other words 'monkey see monkey do'. If you have ever seen, or been part of, a Mexican wave you have witnessed a social contagion at work. Usually initiated by one or a few individuals in a crowd, the wave starts when someone stands up with their arms raised into the air. A few around them copy the movement, and before you know it, the entire crowd co-operates in turn-taking around a stadium, so a wave effect is formed by people obediently leaping out of their seats at precisely the right time. No verbal communication takes place, no warning is given, it just happens and it is contagious.

Social contagion is also evident across social media and can lead to 'bandwagoning' where girls in particular leap onto the latest fad in a desperate attempt to be included in the group. It may be a political movement, or solidarity with the latest identity group de jour. In a recent discussion with an emergency room doctor, we heard of a worrying new social contagion where adolescent girls were using social media to plan and execute measures of self-harm via cutting with a view to strategically ending up in the same ER room where they could ruminate together over their experiences and 'woeful' existence. Heaven help them if they dared to risk exclusion by expressing an original idea of their own and not succumbing to such a potentially dangerous activity via social media. Over the course of the last decade or so, and in an effort to compete for attention with other girls online, we have witnessed the social contagion phenomenon become particularly prominent in fuelling the spread of eating disorders, anxiety-related disorders and more recently, and perhaps controversially, gender dysphoria.

Fear of missing out is a particularly interesting extension of social contagion. Imagine you see a crowd rushing towards something. Social contagion will likely see you scan the area for possible clues as to what it could be, then join in if you don't have enough information to make a decision. That is, if you're not sure what the deal is, you'll join the rush to find out and take part. Failure to do so could mean you might miss out on anything from receiving a reward to successfully fleeing a danger you currently can't see.

As a social species human beings are wired to follow the group – especially in times of uncertainty. We assume that someone up front knows what they are doing, and so we follow. It's a pretty good survival strategy in real life. We see similar behaviour in schools of fish, flocks of birds and even herds of various mammals. Once a critical mass of the herd decides to move, run or go in a particular direction, the rest blindly follow. And to an extent the assumptions underlying this behaviour are usually valid. For example, if you are a deer and some other deer in your herd spot a predator, they move quickly to an area of safety. You don't know why they're suddenly moving, but you're pretty sure they've got good reason to (why would they seek to put themselves or you in danger?) And so you follow. We see humans engaging in similar behaviours – sometimes quite frenetically. Consider the absolute mayhem at Boxing Day sales for example, and most recently the bizarre toilet paper hoarding at the beginning of the COVID-19 pandemic. Humans like to follow and jump on bandwagons for fear of being left behind, and this is ever present with adolescent girls via social media.

FOMO on social media for teens and young adults tends to manifest as being a factor in motivating young girls to be the first on the 'bandwagon'. They enthusiastically leap onto someone else's idea, platform or agenda to align themselves with others as quickly as possible. Such actions allow individuals to inherit some 'borrowed power' from the original source to propel them into some form of a leadership position. Moreover, teens will literally fall over themselves to become quickly aligned with whatever idea, movement or position that is likely to lead to popularity. What they actually think about the issue is largely irrelevant.

Behavioural Activation Theory

This is where our final psychological concept of interest kicks in called Behavioural Activation Theory. This theory suggests that it is in fact behaviour that dictates belief, not the other way around. You may like to think that the reason you behave in a particular way (recycling, exercising, voting) is because you believe in a range of things (climate change, health, political viewpoints). In other words, thought precedes action. Now that is certainly true. However it always comes as a shock to psychology students when we let them in on a scary little secret … your behaviour also changes your beliefs. Simple experiments asking people to actively and publicly argue a position in opposition to their genuine beliefs have shown that doing so shifts their belief toward the direction of their behaviour. In other words, if we can make you behave, we can make you believe.

Cults employ this tactic brilliantly, often by asking people to engage in a range of increasingly difficult and personally taxing behaviours to increase devotion. Otherwise, why would you be hurting yourself in this fashion if it weren't for the best possible cause? Readers from the human resources field might want to investigate the corporate use of 'illegitimate tasks' for pretty much the same purpose … but we digress.

Perhaps it is helpful to think of Behavioural Activation Theory this way: when the average human engages in a behaviour, especially one that comes at cost to them, they must justify that act to themselves. Otherwise it makes them seem rather silly, doesn't it? Behavioural Activation Theory suggests if we can convince to you engage in behaviour A, no matter how ridiculous, a small part of you will attempt to justify why behaviour A is indeed correct and warranted. We are going to come back to this concept in the next chapter when we look at social media postings that use their online platforms to publicise thoughts and behaviours, and how that affects (or, dare we say, stunts) identity development. But for now we want to focus on the knock-on effects of Behavioural Activation via social media.

Imagine 15-year-old Sally has posted a meme in favour of a political party. Sally is actually ambivalent about that party, but she is re-posting from an influential instagrammer and Sally has been feeling a bit deflated lately, with not a lot of friends and not a lot of attention, so she's in the mood to boost her social standing via some borrowed power. So she gets in quick to forward the meme. It turns out Sally hits the social jackpot! All of a sudden she is being showered with likes. Everyone loves her! Her dopamine runneth over. She feels included, important, and even a bit clever for being one of the first groupies, if not the original source. Now how do you think Sally feels about that political party? Is it likely that, given the opportunity, Sally would go doorknocking to muster support for that party in the next election?

See how easily human beliefs and opinions about the simplest of things can be escalated via a pathway of rewards and accolades to cement an idea that they didn't really understand or even care about that much in the first place? What does Sally actually stand for? Initially she stood for popularity, a bit of affiliation and an ego boost. Most of the Sallys of the world (and there are a lot of them) don't even know the ins and outs of the idea they support. They've spent zero time engaging in anything remotely close to critical analysis, and haven't bothered to think through the issues. They just wanted to be loved. When a difficult person comes along and asks a hard question about the substance of their 'beliefs' they can't actually answer. The apparent inability to give a coherent answer lies in the fact that the basis of their behaviour wasn't driven by any actual belief. Instead, Sally, like so many others, is likely unaware or unable to fully grasp what the foundations of her beliefs might actually be. Sally was driven to improve her popularity first and mould her beliefs second. In the end, how is she likely to respond when her beliefs are questioned? She will likely have no idea of substance in this situation, and instead be very upset if it appears that her newfound popularity might be threatened.

Now that's not to say people always re-post or support causes for the above reasons. Clearly there are true believers out there who have thought long and hard about their positions. In fact, you can employ a pretty easy tactic to find out who is the leader and who is the follower in these scenarios. Ask a question. Ask them to explain their rationale. And then watch their response. Are they able to articulate an argument for their position? An idea, even a thought? Remember what we discussed in a previous chapter: In this type of situation, people who are frauds react by 'playing the man instead of the ball'. Instead of engaging in reasoned and thoughtful discourse about the issue, they react instinctively and angrily (as anyone does when they feel threatened) and they shoot the messenger.

In situations similar to Sally's, it is also a major concern if they are found out – because they can't actually articulate why they agree with an idea, they just rushed thoughtlessly in an effort to beat the tide of FOMO to align themselves with a powerful other and increase their own popularity. Their 'beliefs' are entirely vacuous. And they fear being revealed as an imposter. Add in a bit of faux outrage, and their insistence they are horribly 'offended' and congratulations – they have now become an official 'cry-bully'. By painting oneself as a victim, individuals can turn the tables on a person asking a reasonable and rational question.

This is an old psychological manipulation technique – If my partner was to ask me a reasonable question like "Where were you last night?" and I burst into tears and accuse them of not trusting me – that tends to throw people. The natural response is to back away from the original question, reorient to comforting the upset person, and they quickly learn never to ask a difficult question again. This is actually a type of gaslighting, where a perfectly reasonable question is characterised as an offensive affront because:

a) I can't answer it at all, and/or

b) I can't answer it without revealing myself as stupid, and/or

c) I truly have something to hide.

Such approaches and tactics are now ubiquitous across Twitter, Facebook and Instagram. There's rarely an original idea or critical thought on those platforms. However, such online environments are awash with bandwagoning, passive-aggressive gaslighting and cry-bullies.

This behaviour is now so universal, it has recently seen the loss of professional journalists in the public broadcasting business, unable to mentally weather the constant torrent of abuse when they dare even interview a person the twitterazi has determined should have no voice. In an article published late 2021,[1] ABC journalist Leigh Sales detailed an account of her experiences as a female in public broadcasting. Now for readers unfamiliar, the ABC has been characterised by some as being a more 'left-leaning' news outlet. Like all news outlets they deny this and insist they are balanced and centrist. Suffice to say however, they are certainly not NewsCorp. So you would expect that most of their trolling and complaints come from right-wing fanatics. Think again! In Sales' own words:

> *It is that the bullying and harassment now comes, not in an occasional phone call from a real person, but at a furious pace on social media from politicians' acolytes, lackeys, fans and proxies, mostly – but not always – operating anonymously. It is non-stop, personal, often vile, frequently unhinged and regularly based on fabrications.*

Although Sales states that bullying in social media happens to all journalists, she says the trolls are especially vicious with some:

> *All the women face sexual insults and there is a corresponding pattern of racism for reporters of colour.*

Although in the real world, like other ABC journalists, she says she is targeted for criticism by the right of politics, on social media it is a different story.

> *Let's not duck the common thread here — it is overwhelmingly left-leaning Twitter users who are targeting ABC journalists for abuse. Of course, there are right-wing attacks too but the most ferocious campaigns are reserved for any journalist who questions, in even the most anodyne manner, the policies or public statements of Labor politicians.*

We will deal with extremism in the next chapter, but make no mistake, people on both sides of the political fence are equally capable of becoming fanatical and abusive in dictating their worldview. Left-wing authoritarianism is lately a research interest for political psychologists, alarmed at the ways in which this new force is attempting to shut down any kind of speech that disagrees with their point of view.

The differences, as Sales points out, is that these new mob attacks are frequently anonymous and personal. Does this ring any bells from the previous two chapters? Instead of knowing your enemy and being able to have a transparent, face-to-face debate, we must now deal with hidden, passive-aggressive and deeply personal attacks that don't even relate to the substance of the actual topic under consideration. The cry-bully eventually wins when their target is successfully cancelled, or withdraws out of sheer mental exhaustion.

Autistification of a Generation

"The fanatics are the violent ones, the ones who want to change you by force. The ones who will force you to change. They love you. They love you dearly. They love you more than they love themselves. The fanatic has no private life. He or she is one hundred per cent public. No private life. The fanatic gives no value to his or her life. He is eager to sacrifice his life for the sake of a cause, whatever cause, because he doesn't think much of his life. His life is empty. No family, no relationship, no warmth, no human touch to his life. One hundred per cent public."

— Amos Oz[1]

Where Have all our Social Skills Gone?

Those of us who have been on the planet longer than Facebook have noticed some weirdness going on with 'young people these days'. Now we must remind ourselves that older generations historically despair at what they see as faults in the younger. As Aristotle said:

> *They [young people] have exalted notions, because they have not yet been humbled by life or learnt its necessary limitations; moreover, their hopeful disposition makes them think themselves equal to great things ... They would always rather do noble deeds than useful ones: their lives are regulated more by moral feeling than by reasoning; and whereas reasoning leads us to choose what is useful, moral goodness leads us to choose what is noble. They are fonder of their friends, intimates, and companions than older men are, because they like spending their days in the company of others, and have not yet come to value either their friends or anything else by their usefulness to themselves. All their mistakes are in the direction of doing things excessively and vehemently ... they love too much and hate too much, and the same thing with everything else. They think they know everything, and are always quite sure about it; this, in fact, is why they overdo everything.*[2]

Of course, Aristotle has a fair point. He often does! Most would agree that time allows for a certain temperance and balance of one's emotions and hopefully the development of a more rounded, inclusive worldview. However, the current generation (the so-called millennials and younger) are participating in an interesting experiment in that they are the first to have developed their growing brains in an increasingly hybrid world of reality and online environments. It is also significant to recall important points made earlier including that that the human brain wires itself according to the environment in which it finds itself. It is this remarkable capacity that has allowed human beings to thrive in strikingly different environments and spread in plague proportions across the world. Relatedly, our brains 'prune' away unnecessary neurons from puberty until we are in our mid-twenties, leaving only those useful for survival and functioning within our own particular social and cultural milieu. Therefore humans can learn to survive along the equator as well as in the cold and forbidding environment of the North Pole. No other species has achieved this feat. It's down to our remarkably adaptive big brains that are shaped to deal with the particular environmental conditions we find ourselves in.

The same notions of adaptability can be applied to our social skills. Adolescence is the time when that over-emotional and somewhat reckless brain kicks into full gear to develop peer relationships that will drive future romantic pairings, and hopefully form the basis of a new generation of thinkers and leaders. A key question, then, is what happens in the developing brains of young people when those social skills are forming online? The true answer is, we don't yet know. But we have some recent research that gives us cause for concern.

Let's start at the beginning. Heffler and colleagues[3] recently published research that demonstrated higher television and video exposure and less in-real-life play placed one-year-olds at greater risk of displaying 'ASD-like symptoms'. They asked parents fairly basic questions about their infants' abilities such as: Does your child look you in the eye? Does your child ever pretend? Does your child imitate you? Does your child sometime stare at nothing and wander with no purpose? Does your child seem oversensitive to noise? and so on. Even in the first year of life, over-exposure to screens and under-exposure to in-real-life interactions made these infants resemble toddlers with autism. In 2021, different researchers found that the amount of time spent on a screen device had a significant association with deficits in social skill development and having autism spectrum disorder-like symptoms in four to six year olds.[4] It's important to pause here to clarify that we are not suggesting that using a screen device is going to make your child autistic, as correlation does not equal causation. There is however, a relationship here worthy of further investigation.

Autism expert Yalda Uhls[5] had earlier sounded the warning on this possible developmental trajectory where 'neurotypical' children were displaying autistic like behaviours thanks to over-exposure to screens. That peer reviewed research looked at the impact of removing screens from pre-teens for five days and sending them off to nature camp. Compared to controls, removing screen time from pre-teens for barely a week markedly increased their social interaction skills and improved their non-verbal recognition skills.

There are now a smorgasbord of individual research studies demonstrating a link between screen usage and autistic-like behaviours. And the results should come as no surprise. If you displace in-real-life activities that build social learning and interpersonal skills with shallow yet entertaining screen-based dopamine hits, you are unlikely to develop the social sophistication required to navigate real life interactions. Simply stated, screen time is numbing the mind and particularly impedes the development of recognition skills for emotions that form the basis of non-verbal communication.

The knock-on effects of stunted socio-emotional communication are yet to be fully realised. However, it seems reasonable to speculate that friendship formation, building strong social bonds and essentially playing well with others will be negatively affected. In the end, many aspects of wellbeing are likely to be diminished as children struggle to form and maintain the types of social connections necessary to act as a buffer to psychosocial disorders. Uhls, writing in *The Lancet*,[5] confirmed what we've all seen anecdotally – that mental wellbeing in adolescents has "declined considerably during past decades" and noted evidence of detrimental impacts of screen time on mental wellbeing that started at just one hour per day.

Let's focus here on non-verbal recognition skills, because verbal dialogue makes up an approximate of 10% of what we express in any one interaction, while body language, facial expressions, posture, possibly even pheromones give away far more. It's no wonder secret agents are specifically trained to recognise 'microexpressions'. So just think about that for a minute – what happens when you are missing 90% of what's actually being said? You've just put yourselves in the shoes of a person with autism. People with ASD have enormous trouble discerning anything other than direct verbal or written statements (and often even those as well). Hence their tendency to take everything literally. They can miss sarcasm, jokes, and especially misconstrue a situation where what is said doesn't match the actual feeling behind it (e.g. she smiled through gritted teeth). As one of our mature age students with ASD commented:

Imagine walking into a room and everyone is wearing the same face mask. That's all I see, I don't know what they're thinking until they start speaking. And even then I get into trouble because I think I'm going along with a joke ... and then I get the punch to the head.

Aside from intentional punches to the head, so many of our daily interactions are largely intuitive, and those of us raised in-real-life now take for granted our second-nature emotion recognition skills. But these were not with us a birth; they were shaped and honed, as our neurons were pruned and tuned to better discern what was really going on with other people around us. This taken-for-granted process of emotional development is necessary for us to become mentally healthy and socially functioning human beings and plays a role in so much of what we do, especially in terms of relationships. Friendship formation, for example, relies on intimacy-building; the capacity to understand and honestly reciprocate another's interest in you. This is what relationship researchers sometimes call connection or chemistry. Imagine the fall-out if you keep getting this wrong, sometimes even causing inadvertent offence. Far fewer friends, for a start.

In terms of supporting healthy development, an inability to understand another's perspective, which has become another defining feature of younger generations, can create numerous problems. So much so that the United Kingdom now has a Minister for Loneliness. Hardly surprising in a world where people are becoming less equipped to build and maintain friendships, because they simply lack the learned ability to do so.

Notwithstanding the challenges arising from a decline in the ability to view things from different perspectives, researchers who have been studying generational changes are also noting some consistent patterns. The generational decline in perspective taking ability parallels a generational increase in narcissism. This is thought to be due, in some part at least, to a shift of values away from community and social affiliations, to money, fame and image. Narcissism leads to declines in prosocial behaviour and less civic engagement (interest in social issues, government, and politics) and further reduces the opportunity for social connections that build perspective taking.

An inability to make social connections and friends, along with increases in narcissism, requires us to consider what might be contributing to such worrying phenomena. Some research supports the proposition that social media has impacted perspective-taking due to the digital algorithms that foster confirmation and form online silos where we only see and hear from people who think the same as we do. Whistleblower Frances Haugen[6] confirmed that Facebook was little more than an echo chamber that deliberately sent polarising information to solidify already held views and promote in-group/out-group thinking. So imagine a teen sitting at their computer, whipping themselves into a frenzy about the latest social issue – fed by the algorithms of Facebook to dumb down any alternative perspective lest it lead to some critical thinking or, heaven forbid, empathy for another's position. One could even suggest that this is a form of 'personal fake news'!

This inability to tolerate another's point of view – ironically in a generation that likes to trot out 'inclusivity' and 'diversity' at every virtue signalling opportunity – has led to some spectacular fallouts.

In previous chapters we touched on protests, de-platforming and all manner of incredible reactions to a position that is not 100% in favour of the mob. But what about on the home front?

Being the old fogeys we are, we remember with a sense of bewildered bemusement the fracture caused in the UK during the Brexit vote. Now, neither of us have any expert understanding of the issues between the EU and UK, but what was of interest to us was the impact at ground level of this (non)debate on everyday families. Young people started to decry that they could no longer look their grandparents in the eye or maintain friendships with others who voted contrary to their belief! One of us is married to a partner who votes for a different political party – in fact, we both belong to a generation where this is not uncommon. And yet, here were young people in their droves de-platforming grandma and de-friending anyone in their peer group who didn't vote for their preferred outcome! We cannot begin to impart how bizarre this looked from one generation to the next. It is small wonder people are unable to maintain friendships and keep family bonds together, when a political disagreement is enough to see the non-believers excommunicated permanently. The mind boggles as to how anyone with this fixed and rigid attitude could successfully keep a long-term marriage together, or tolerate children who, horror of horrors, might grow up with a mind of their own.

The rifts amongst family members during Brexit were also certainly not helped outside one's individual echo chamber. Among all the articles splashed across the British media, hand-wringing about how one could never speak to another again (on the basis of political difference!), never did we see any attempt to actually understand the other's point of view. They were immediately branded racist or any other kind of 'ist' you care to nominate and sentenced without trial to a hated out-group.

From a psychological point of view – herein lies the problem – even if we disagree most vehemently with a person's perspective, failure to at least attempt to understand why a person thinks that way removes the opportunity for a meaningful and constructive dialogue that might ultimately pave the way for mind-change, compromise, or at the very least some empathy. It is possible to disagree very strongly with another's point of view, and yet have empathy for it. We might disagree strongly with another's decision to steal. But in listening to their rationale (even if we disagree with that as well) we can build understanding and empathise with the circumstances or background that led them to this point. We can still say, hand on heart, we wouldn't have done the same in their situation, but we can see why they made that decision. This doesn't mean we agree with stealing, or condone it, or think they have a reasonable excuse. But opening your heart and mind to try to discern the motives of others will build your own Theory of Mind and broaden your perspectives. There is a lot of wisdom in the old saying: you have one mouth and two ears – use in proportion.

We posit that all parents should be concerned with any signs that their children are withdrawing from the world, thinking only of themselves (always) and seeking out like-minded tribal bonds. Perspective taking and empathy building has become yet another casualty in the millennials and minus generations. Instead of working through difficult scenarios and complex problems in real life, with their peers, it's much easier to log onto social media and be fed a pile of misrepresentations by an algorithm designed to momentarily bolster their feeling of social inclusion. This also has an impact on how a young person views themselves and their place in the world.

Identity and the Self

Who are you? How do you see yourself? Are you the same person in public, in private, with friends, family or at work? Whilst it might seem on face value that consistency is a good thing, think again. Would you honestly admit some of your deepest feelings to your work colleague, friend, even partner? How about to yourself? How many secrets of the self do you hold?

Intimacy-building relies on the revelation of yourself, your real self, your beliefs, feelings and desires to another who accepts, values and maybe even reciprocates your thoughts. In the film *Avatar*, the Na'vi did not profess love for one another, but professed a simpler but more profound 'I see you'. 'Seeing' into another person's innermost self is the basis for our strongest intimate partnerships.

Psychological researcher Harry Triandis pondered the difference between a 'public' and 'private' self that we all embody. Most people can relate to keeping their real opinions or values to themselves while in public or in an unknown group of people. We lay off any tawdry jokes, un-PC opinions or bad language until we get to know those around us. Once we are confident that our sense of humour or manner of speaking won't be misunderstood, and will be appreciated, we start to reveal ourselves bit by bit in a socially acceptable manner. All the while, we engage our emotion recognition radar to determine how our expressions are being received. It's only in our most intimate relationships with deep connections that we can truly be ourselves. This is the person we are in the wee small hours of the morning when we think about life's issues.

Thinking of 'ourselves' is important and the impetus for the opening quote of this chapter. The late Amos Oz grew up in war-torn Jerusalem and developed a profound insight into where extremist thinking leads. Interestingly, he may well have prophesised the impact of increased polarisation and the loss of your true or 'private' self in today's social media environment. Oz hypothesised that terrorists and other extremists lack a private self. This is a really interesting way of framing this behaviour. Your private self is the part of you used for quiet reflection, learning and mind change. So what happens to that teenager who raises themself and 'develops' their opinions on social media?

If your opinions are made public the second they bubble up from your undeveloped brain – what kind of thinking do we see? Black and white opinions – fiercely defended. Typical for the teen brain, in fact. No shades of grey and little open-mindedness. Ideas are limited to an 150-character tweet, compounded with poor attention and concentration, which leaves little room for deep reflection and critical thinking. When does today's teenager have the opportunity for self-reflection, learning and mind-change while existing in a 24/7 Matrix of anonymity and misinformation? And remember, this occurs in a virtual world where signalling one's virtue and seeking affirmation is prolific; a world very different from previous generations.

Ask yourself, what embarrassing ideologies or beliefs did you harbour across your lifespan? Especially during your teenage years when your brain was still developing? Many a celebrity, sportsperson and politician has become unstuck when an old tweet, social media post or drunken blackface at a party has popped up thanks to the eternal lifespan of servers. People have lost livelihoods and careers for posting something stupid as a teenager or young adult. All we can say to that is there but for the grace of good luck would go all of us. Those who earnestly believe they are in a position to cast the first stone on this issue almost certainly fit into Oz's definition of a fanatic.

Remember, the fanatic has no private life, no relationship, no warmth and is 100% public with a desire to force you to change! So think for just a minute – what is a person's first response when attacked? To defend? That would certainly be the norm. So if you hold an idea that doesn't stack up well to analysis, but now you've blasted it out publicly, what can you do? Do you dig your heels in and defend further, or do you back down and apologise profusely for fear of being yet another victim of the cry-bullies? Either way, did your mobbing genuinely cause you to reflect, ponder and change your mind? Or did it:

- cement your position further; and/or
- make you more mindful of presenting a public self that is totally at odds with your private self – otherwise known as being inauthentic or a fraud?

The thought and behaviour police, especially on social media, are becoming increasingly voracious. Some Dr Seuss books have been banned. (Those who don't understand the magnitude of this from a historical perspective might like to look up book-burning.) Sportspeople are being forced against their will to make public displays in favour of political positions. Regardless of whether they agree with said position or not, is it ever OK to force people to do so when their job is to chase a ball around a field? But as Oz correctly predicted, all of this is being done for our own good! Those who drive this love us all and need to protect us from ourselves! For many young people who have a diminished capacity for looking at things from various perspectives due to a brain that has been trained to do otherwise, the road to speaking and acting without thinking and reflection is not only problematic for the individual but also for the social and cultural milieu in which they exist.

We live in increasingly dangerous times for free speech as the extremists leak into surprising avenues of thought and debate to shut it all down. Again, even if you disagree vehemently with what is being said, what is the outcome of banning thought and speech? We already know that in most instances, you simply drive dangerous ideas underground where they fester, and their proponents become increasingly incensed by the message they receive that somehow they are 'lesser' for believing them. Robust debates or fierce conversations, even of unpalatable ideas, are the only way to air them. Attempted suppression often does little but give them fertilizer to propagate further. As Martin Luther King Jr said:

Darkness cannot drive out darkness; only light can do that.

We don't yet fully understand or know what life on social media does to the developing identity, but we only need look to current events to see a range of psychological processes playing out in ways that while not unforeseen, perhaps were underestimated. Lack of perspective taking, empathy building and a total unwillingness to engage in an idea or position that isn't the popularity bolster de jour, is shaping a generation of 'sheeple' incapable of critical thought and self-reflection.

We openly speculate that social media may be creating a form of identity 'stunting', that is, teens bandwagon into groups and become increasingly tribal instead of having the opportunity to genuinely develop their own identity. Now to a degree, this has always been the case. (Sports jocks versus nerds anyone?)

Identity development has been considered the core psychological business of adolescence. This is where you decide who you are, what you stand for, what you want out of life. It's actually a thrilling time! But what happens if that individual development is thwarted or hijacked? Remember the process of Behavioural Activation (if you behave it you believe it)? Teens find themselves leaping onto ideologies fed to them via marketing algorithms. The nature of tweeting and snapchatting is all about instant recognition. There is little appetite for thoughtful mulling of ideas and the development of critical thinking, let alone mind-change. How do you back away from such publicly proclaimed opinions? And so identity politics has become the new gang-related crime! Instead of making mistakes, rethinking, reflecting and analysing to forge their own identity, teens addicted to social media are lost in a Matrix of narcissism, numb to the real world around them and unable to connect. A generation, who for all intent and purposes, is showing the behaviours of an autistic mind. The question then, is what, if anything, can be done to diffuse this and promote healthy development.

Get Out and Get Real – Nature as a Buffer to All Things Virtual

"If, when we were young, we tramped through the forests of Nebraska cottonwoods, or raised pigeons on the rooftop in Queens, or fished for Ozark bluegills, or felt the swell of a wave that travelled a thousand miles before lifting our boat, then we were bound to the natural world and remain so today. Nature still informs our years – lifts us, carries us."

— Richard Louv[1]

Nature still informs our years – lifts us, carries us. How many of today's techno-generation might be able to claim this now or as they grow older? As we have noted throughout this book, from early childhood through adolescence, young people are increasingly relying on screens devices for information, entertainment and social interactions. This reliance on, and attachment to, screens means they are existing in autistic-like states of sedentary isolation. It is our contention that this is not only unhealthy both physically and mentally but, importantly, can be easily remedied with the help of Mother Nature. The evidence for such a claim is abundant and unambiguous.

Prior to looking at the evidence noted earlier, it is important to reiterate that we are not 'luddites' advocating for a return to some notion of a golden era of technology free utopia. Nor do we seriously believe that it would be advantageous, or realistic, to condemn smartphones or any form of screen device to some historical heap of irrelevance. We are social scientists who study and research aspects of child and adolescent development. We are interested in what impacts on young people, both positively and negatively and we do not hold any grudges, malicious intent or ill will towards those companies and people who have given us the power of a super-computer in the palm of our hand; this is not an 'us versus them' situation. However, and in the immortal words of Peter Parker's Uncle Ben in the first ever *Spiderman* movie, "with great power comes great responsibility." It is our contention that the seemingly divine glow of technology has blinded many to accepting any responsibility in terms of understanding what might be happening to a generation of children and teens whose brains are malleable and shaped by the environment, both actual and virtual. Fortunately, the techno challenges described throughout this book can be met by reclaiming some balance, and guiding young people to one of the brain's most cherished places ... the natural environment.

Reclaiming a Balance, Naturally!

There is a wealth of evidence linking the need for human beings to connect with nature and the healing properties associated with a range of outdoor activities. From the outset, a sceptic might question such a claim but it is the biophilia hypothesis that helps us understand our connection to the natural world. The concept of biophilia suggests that as living beings, we share an inherent connection with all other living matter. When we attempt to replace those connections with artificial pretenders (e.g. living in a built environment, replacing real human interactions with digital 'friends'), we thwart innate biological needs, leading to a range of dysfunctional mental processes. Psychological researcher Harry Harlow and his colleagues were some of the first researchers to look into the connections that bind people and animals together in ways that continue to prove difficult for scientific analysis. For example, it is difficult to measure the 'chemistry' or 'spark' that ignites a connection among some lovers, yet remains elusive to observers, even though those lovers do look good as a couple. After all, how do you measure falling, and staying, in love? Harlow, however, gave us some very interesting insights into the love that binds a mother and baby.

By today's standards, Harlow's work would be considered too cruel to gain approval from peers and research approval boards. His infamous monkey experiments effectively removed baby monkeys from their mothers and offered them a substitute in her place. One substitute was a wire monkey that held a bottle full of milk (clearly something necessary for a hungry or starving monkey) while the other offering was a warm and cuddly teddy-bear-type replica of their mother. Inexplicably and irrationally, the hungry baby monkeys refused the food from the cold wire mother substitute, and instead sought comfort from the warm and welcoming avatar.[2] Tragically, Harlow's baby monkeys did not do well and without their mother they all eventually went 'mad'. The innate need to be connected to another, even in human beings, has been replicated many times since Harlow's work with primates. We now know that humans have evolved to be social creatures and relationships are important to mind and body alike. Social isolation is a recipe for all types of illness and screens offer social isolation vis-à-vis extended time in a virtual world at the expense of being connected to the real one. Importantly, the real world, and in particular, the natural environment offers a context for restoring wellbeing in children and teens. Plenty of studies have demonstrated that connecting with nature is intrinsically motivating, enjoyable, and can reduce negative emotions while increasing more positive emotional states ... in short, Mother Nature can heal us.[3]

In 1984, psychologist Roger Ulrich published a curious finding: patients recovering in hospital rooms that were afforded a view of green spaces got better quicker, and with less intervention, than those confined to a room facing bricks and mortar.[4] Since that time, researchers from a diverse range of professions have empirically demonstrated the healing effect of exposure to nature, and have attempted to better understand the mechanisms behind its restorative properties. So a good question might be, what is it about green spaces that make us feel good and can improve our overall wellbeing?

The type of experiments that have followed this work help to highlight an innate and inherent need for living things to connect with other living things, and remind us that artificial substitutes hold little value. Attention Restoration Theory (ART) and Stress Recovery Theory (SRT) offer a platform for understanding how nature appears to exert an array of healing properties. First coined by Rachel and Stephen Kaplan, ART suggests that man-made objects are more cognitively taxing to process compared to natural objects (hard edges, geometric shapes). In other words, the built environment is harder for us to process in our minds as our subconscious struggles with those things that are not natural. For example, next time you are in a dense urban environment, stop and consider how comfortable you feel immersed in concrete and steel with sharp angles, cold facades or bright neon lights. A conscious focus on such infrastructure can lead to cognitive overload and attention fatigue but we can also tire from such elements without thinking of them and being simply immersed in those spaces. However, according to ART, the simple opportunity of experiencing nature scenes and elements, especially water features though exposure to natural environments, can help in diminishing such over-load and fatigue.[5] These insights have fostered the term 'soft fascination' as a way of recognising that natural environments are not cognitively taxing to look at and provide opportunities for reflection, and a form of restorative practice for alleviating attention fatigue.[6]

In a similar fashion to ART, SRT taps into the field of evolutionary psychology and suggests that human beings are biologically primed to feel better in natural, vegetation-rich environments.[7] Both theories have been built upon by numerous other researchers and there is little doubt that being in nature has therapeutic benefits.[8] This is good news for those young people whose minds have been temporarily wired into a daydream-like state of disassociation with reality through constant screen consumption. For you, the reader, another important question might be whether there is any evidence of the positive impact of nature on the developing brain of your children, and the short answer is yes!

Although in its infancy, research is getting closer to understanding the mechanisms by which exposure to nature can, in fact, change the trajectory of the developing brain. With the young brain's neuroplasticity at its highest, exposure to nature is showing promise in increasing growth in brain areas associated with better attentional control. Looking at the other side of the equation, screen time continues to show both behavioural and neurological changes associated with both ADHD and autism-like symptoms. Relatedly, and central to the fundamental message in this book, are the key points that the human brain does not fully mature until the third decade of life, that the brains of children and teens are highly vulnerable to environmental influences and that technology may be shaping young people's brains to operate in an attention-deficit and autistic like manner.

Furthermore, and in an effort to keep our children safe, we have counterproductively introduced a downstream raft of highly problematic outcomes by limiting childhood exposure to the natural environment. In one short generation we've gone from 73% to 13% of children spending more time playing outside than inside, with only one in five of today's children having climbed a tree.[9] Currently, maximum-security prisoners are mandated to have more outside time than the average Australian child spends outdoors, with obvious implications. This has seen the rise in a new term to help explain the counter-intuitive rise in a variety of anxiety and stress related disorders during a time when Western affluence has given children greater measure of safety, security and opportunity – Nature Deficit Disorder. So what can be, and should be done?

Treating Nature Deficit Disorder

From the outset it is important to reiterate that we cannot create an experiment where we purposefully expose children to excessive screen use and deprive them of the outdoors to try and exactly measure what damage is done and then see if we can fix it. We can, however, look at research findings that have demonstrated the healing properties of natural environments in children diagnosed with various disorders and similar findings where the outdoors has had measurable impact on various aspects of development. Such findings, outlined in examples below, tell us that we should do all we can to alleviate Nature Deficit Disorder by getting children away from their screen devices and out into the natural world.

In 2008, researchers found that children clinically diagnosed with ADHD could concentrate better after a 20 minute walk in the park![10] In this study the children with ADHD completed a series of tests before and after they walked through three different environments one week apart. One walk was through a vegetation-rich urban park while the other two were through the streets of a downtown area and an area clustered with houses respectively. After each walk, various aspects of attention and executive functioning were tested and walking through the park showed much better performance on those tests than walking in the other environments. In fact, walking through nature showed comparable results on tests of attention to other children who had taken the tests while medicated with methylphenidate or what is commonly known as Ritalin. The researchers concluded that doses of nature might serve as a safe, inexpensive, widely accessible non-medical tool for managing ADHD.[11]

In a more recent study of more than 900,000 people published in 2019, researchers found that those who had access to a large amount of green space where they lived during childhood were significantly less likely to be at risk of developing psychiatric disorders, regardless of other risk factors.[12] In short, living within areas with a great deal of green spaces contributed to better mental health for those individuals across the lifespan. There are an abundance of other studies that corroborate those findings. For example, there is evidence showing that childhood exposure to green spaces and the natural environment can be linked to fewer depressive symptoms in adulthood, fewer emotional problems during childhood, better measures of emotional wellbeing than those resulting from moderate-to-vigorous physical activity, and for those concerned with the health of the planet, a greater emotional affinity to, and desire for, protecting biodiversity.[13] We also know that if we let children outside to play and do so without adult interference or risk averse sanitisation of the environment, the benefits are substantive, go beyond wellbeing and include such things as building competence and autonomy.

Gaining Control Makes for Better Minds

One of the truisms of ageing is that as we grow older and begin to navigate our environments with increased sophistication, the majority of humans get a kick out of feeling effective and in control of themselves in their surroundings. Remember the look of glee on your child's face when they took their first steps as a toddler or mastered riding a bicycle without training wheels?

Most humans also prefer to exercise free will in choosing activities that appeal to them. Remember those two crucial factors in building psychological wellbeing referred to by psychologists as 'competence' and 'autonomy'? The kind of experiences that help cultivate the development of both competence and autonomy are found via a moderately but genuinely challenging environment, where kids can test their abilities in self-assessment, problem-solving, risk-taking, and adaptation in response to challenge and failure. These experiences are particularly crucial during critical or sensitive periods when the brain is most receptive to such stimulation, and such experiences are in abundance in the natural environment or those that embody some degree of 'risky business'.

Adults need to remember that any challenge generally comes with some measure of inherent risk. Occasionally that risk can be quite traumatic (e.g., a broken limb, concussion). However, and contrary to popular belief, research has shown that the hyper-sanitised, risk-averse play culture we have lately created for our children may well be counterproductive. When the Sydney Playground Project released children into a playground with 44-gallon drums, old milk cartons, ropes and other certain 'death traps' as perceived by adults, they observed a reduction in fighting and bullying amongst children.[14] These results were supported by New Zealand research that demonstrated a drop in serious injuries (along with bullying) when the playground 'rule book' created by adults was thrown out.[15] Why? Because kids can, and will, learn to take responsibility for their own safety if you let them. They, like most other mammals, also thrive through peer interactions where social competence is fostered by utilising perhaps the greatest teaching tool ever to acquire such information – play![16]

Play is important and when parents withhold from their children the opportunity to take risks, to learn from failure, to discover coping techniques that are adaptive and problem-focussed, they withhold the opportunity for their children to learn. Children's growing brains fail to develop autonomy, competence, self-discipline, good decision-making, good self-assessment of ability, high failure tolerance, and a range of other cognitive and psychological benefits. In hyper-sanitary play experiences, adults 'hardwire' children to become psychologically fragile, fearful, avoidant and helpless in the face of challenge and failure rather than facilitating their opportunities to innovate, problem-solve, bounce back from failure and adapt as they go forth to meet life's inevitable challenges.

You might be thinking whether we are overstating the need for unsupervised play. We would ask you to consider that the safety pendulum has swung too far to one side in an effort to protect children from all risk and harm to the point that when they do enter adulthood, they feel everything is a threat, that they need 'safe' spaces and where words are violence.[17] This is compounded by children spending more and more time on screens in perhaps the most sterile and sanitised environment for a young developing mind. Furthermore, too much time on screens makes children sanitised and sterile versions of themselves, willing to have their identity potentially shaped in an unhealthy context. Such children would benefit from time in the parental embrace of the natural environment.

Mother Nature is a seriously tough-love parent and can seem unforgiving at times. Sticks and stones can indeed break some bones but such events are rare given the resilient nature of the human body. Relatedly, the psychological benefit arising from sticks and stones lies in the fact that in the face of challenge and failure in the natural environment, children will learn important skills of adaptation and emotional regulation – which in short, will put some fight in the dog. So, is it time to take stock and ask yourself if you and your children need to restore a more balanced experience, utilising the outdoors, for their developing brains?

A good first step in considering the best environment for children might be to try and determine how artificial is the totality of the environment that your children experience every day. Is their world a concrete jungle and/or predominantly the work of human ingenuity or do they have a great deal of time in green spaces devoid of risk-averse playground equipment? Are they encouraged, or forced, to spend time away from the screen devices that are designed to act like digital cocaine? Is consideration given to ensuring that the balance between social media and real time friends swings towards being with real people in real time?

It is time for parents to take stock of their children's virtual lives and arrest potential issues before they manifest into full-blown disorders. For those who are in the midst of having to deal with young people who have suddenly, and seemingly out of nowhere, become transfixed with virtual worlds and lost in the Matrix, it is important to remember that the prescription or cure for any virus of the mind resulting from an excess of screen time and withdrawing from reality can simply be found by spending time in the natural world. It turns out that being in the grasp of Mother Nature for:

- 20 minutes per week lowers stress;[18]
- 30 minutes per week lowers blood pressure and risks of depression;[19]
- 90 minutes per week reduces rumination or the constant internal gazing of negative emotions;[20] and
- 120 minutes or more per week results not only in better physical health but also in numerous measure of overall mental wellbeing.[21]

The jury is out(doors)! The alluring virtual world that grasps the minds of children and adolescents alike, and renders them out of touch with the real world, can be balanced with the help of the natural environment. The vacuous stare and inability to connect with others because of too much time in a virtual world can be healed by spending greater time with people in the real world and most notably in the real 'natural' world whenever possible.

It is apparent that exposure to nature has transitioned from a wellbeing movement to a bona fide scientific endeavour. So much so we can now move to specific 'prescriptions' for whatever ails us and our children. As researchers inch closer to understanding the mechanisms of change, we strongly suggest that we know enough now, especially in the context of the developing brain, to ensure that a child's exposure to play opportunities in nature is considered as one of the basic necessities for optimal growth and development. It is perhaps no coincidence that top software developers in Silicon Valley obtained notoriety in recent years for banning their own children from using various devices, which subsequently saw the rise of 'low-tech' schools in the United States and abroad. When the designers of such technologies see fit to withhold their creative inventions from their own children, you can be sure they know something we don't. As parents, caregivers, teachers and healthcare providers, we have the opportunity now to learn from past mistakes. Recent insights from research has given us a better understanding of the importance of offering a greener future to our children, so that nature may lift them and carry them to a better state of mind. In the end, however, it will be up to you to take stock of the environment in which your child or children spend most of their time and alter that environment when necessary to ensure that that generation is not on a virtual pathway to *'becoming autistic'*.

Be Concerned and Vigilant, But Not Afraid!

"Open the newspaper, watch the evening news. On any given day, there's a good chance that someone – a journalist, activist, consultant, corporate executive, or politician – is warning about an 'epidemic' of something or other that threatens you and those you hold dear."

— Daniel Gardner[1]

When we set out to write this book we thought long and hard about the research we were going to use, the content we were going to include or omit and the overall intent in sharing our expertise. We have spent many collective years crafting our scholarly and academic identities and as such are always mindful that there will be those who endorse and accept our ideas but equally, those who look to refute our position.

This was also at the forefront of our minds when we chose to use 'Becoming Autistic' as the title of this book. We are not suggesting that using a screen device is going to make your child autistic. It is safe to say that screen devices are here to stay and will only change in function and sophistication. Equally so, there are patterns of maturation in children that have evolved in humans over a very long time and are still necessary for healthy, normal, social and emotional development. We've used the words 'evolutionary psychology' a few times throughout this book. It's worth remembering that evolution is a very slow beast; minute changes via natural selection take hundreds if not thousands of years. Think then about the rapid changes over the last two centuries and the explosion in technology in just the last couple of decades. It's hardly surprising our brains are struggling to keep up.

Being with others, playing in groups and engaging with all aspects of the real world, especially the outdoors, are important components of a developing mind and body. We have tried to highlight the benefits of such activities as a remedy for emerging behaviours that resemble those found in individuals with a degree of autism or, at the very least, as a tool for ensuring young people grow up healthy and in a healthy environment. An underlying assumption of such an approach is not to look at screen time solutions which may be developmentally appropriate or finding ways to make screens more child friendly but rather to ask parents and caregivers to consider – how do we structure environments to best meet the needs of children and teens?[2]

Increasingly, more and more studies are pointing to a wide variety of issues and challenges related to healthy development at the intersection of technological advances. We know, for example, that electronic communication is linked to poor mental health while interacting in person is linked to good mental health; the two types of engagement with people are simply not the same.[3] And if a global pandemic has taught us one thing with a degree of certainty, it is that social isolation, regardless of the myriad of online platforms for connecting with others, can wreak havoc on the minds of young and old alike. Human beings are, by nature, social creatures and flourish in environments with real people in real time. To that end, we hope that after reading the book you can see that our intent has been to give you pause to think that the time children spend on screen devices should be a smaller fraction of their lives than time spent doing so many other things.

Chapter Notes

Introduction
What's Happening to Young Minds?

1. Carr, 2011, p. 207.
2. Heying & Weinstein, 2021.
3. LeDoux, 1998.
4. Heying & Weinstein, 2021, suggest that online pornography produces sexual autism where autism is used metaphorically in this example to show a disconnect between sensory stimulation and social and emotional attachment.

Chapter 1
Imagining the Unimaginable

1. Diamond & Hopson, 1999.
2. LeDoux, 1998.

3. Nagel & Scholes, 2016; see also Carter, 2009; Sweeney, 2009; D'angelo, 2019.
4. Herculano-Houzel, 2009.
5. Nagel & Scholes, 2016; see also Berninger & Richards, 2002; Herschkowitz & Herschkowitz, 2004.
6. Stoodley, 2016.
7. Gold & Toomey, 2018.
8. Nagel, 2012.
9. Mitchell, 2018.
10. Nagel & Scholes, 2016; see also Pinker, 2002; Bjorklund, 2005; Nagel, 2012.
11. Pinker, 2002.
12. Voss et al., 2017.
13. Mitchell, 2018.
14. Pinker, 2002, p. 86.
15. Eagleman, 2020, p. 14.
16. Kim et al., 2018.

Chapter 2
This is the Brain on Adolescence!

1. Dahl, 2003, p. 8.
2. Hall, 1904, Volume 1, p. xiii.
3. Arnett, 1999, p. 317.
4. Nagel, 2014; see also Arnett, 1999; Masten et al., 1999, 2012; Dahl, 2004; Steinberg et al., 2006.
5. Wilbrecht, 2018; for insights into differences evident through scanning see Giedd et al., 1996; Giedd, 2004; Durston et al., 2006.
6. As discussed in Bryson, 2019. For a full copy of Professor Jensen's commentary see Ruder, 2008.
7. Nagel, 2012.
8. Cuzzolin et al., 2020.
9. Nagel, 2014; see also Blakemore, 2008; Sebastian et al., 2012; Weimer et al., 2017.
10. Shamay-Tsoory et al., 2010.

Chapter 3
Entering the Matrix

1. Sugata et al., 2005.
2. Korones, 2012.
3. Wood et al., 2011.
4. Fried, 2008.
5. Organisation For Economic Cooperation and Development (OECD), 2015.
6. Ibid, pp. 3-4.
7. Ibid, p. 162.
8. Hattie, 2013.
9. Borst et al., 2010.
10. Wood et al., 2011.
11. See Twenge 2017 for an expansive and authoritative list of challenges and issues related to screen use, children and adolescents.
12. Kakabadse et al., 2009.
13. American Psychiatric Association, 2013.
14. Twenge, 2017.
15. Ibid; Sigman, 2009.
16. Nagel, 2014.

Chapter 4
The Divine Glow of Screens!

1. Royal Life Saving Australia, 2020.
2. Lissak, 2018.

Chapter 5
The Usual Suspects: Violence, addiction, cyberbullying and cybersex

1. Australian Bureau of Statistics, 2018.
2. Social Learning Theory is the product of the work done by Professor Albert Bandura at Stanford University in the 1960s and

early 1970s. For a fuller description of his work see Bandura, 1962, 1977; Bandura & Walters, 1963.
3. American Psychiatric Association, 2013.
4. Vannucci et al., 2017.
5. McNicol & Thorsteinsson, 2017.
6. Twenge et al., 2018.
7. Abi-Jaoude et al., 2020.
8. Marengo et al., 2018.
9. ABC Catalyst, 2011.
10. Child and Youth Mental Health Service (CYMHS), 2014.
11. Buchholz, 2019.
12. Mitchell et al., 2003.
13. Corlett & Crabbe, 2013
14. Horvath et al., 2013.
15. El-Hamamsy et al., 2021.
16. Marston & Lewis, 2014.
17. Tankard-Reist, 2019.

Chapter 6
Social Media or Social Disease – The Girls Are not All Right

1. Sales, 2021.

Chapter 7
Autistification of a Generation

1. Oz, 2001.
2. Aristotle, in Honeycutt, 2004.
3. Heffler et al., 2020.
4. Alrahili et al., 2021.
5. Uhls et al., 2014.
6. Spring, 2021.

Chapter 8
Get Out and Get Real – Nature as a Buffer to All Things Virtual

1. Louv, 2008.
2. Harlow et al., 1965.
3. Tester-Jones et al., 2020.
4. Ulrich, 1984.
5. Kaplan & Kaplan, 1989.
6. Kaplan, 1995.
7. Ulrich 1983; Ulrich et al., 1991.
8. Hartig et al., 2014; Ohly et al., 2016.
9. Planet Ark, 2011.
10. Taylor & Kuo, 2008.
11. Ibid.
12. Engemann et al., 2019.
13. Snell et al., 2016; Soga & Gaston, 2016; Ward et al., 2016; Zach et al., 2016.
14. The Sydney Playground Project, 2017.
15. Hill, 2014.
16. Sapolsky, 2017.
17. Heying & Weinstein, 2021.
18. Hunter et al., 2019.
19. Shanahan et al., 2016.
20. Bratman et al., 2015.
21. White et al., 2019.

Conclusion
Be Concerned and Vigilant, But Not Afraid!

1. Gardner, 2009, p. 6.
2. Owenz, 2021.
3. Twenge, 2017.

Bibliography

Abi-Jaoude, E., Naylor, K. & Pignatiello, A. (2020). Smartphones, social media use and youth mental health. CMAJ: *Canadian Medical Association journal = journal de l'Association medicale canadienne,* 192(6), E136–E141. <https://doi.org/10.1503/cmaj.190434>.

ABC Catalyst (2011). Mean Girls. <https://www.abc.net.au/catalyst/mean-girls/11012748>.

Alrahili, N., Almarshad, N., Alturki, R., Alothaim, J., Altameem, R., Alghufaili, M., Alghamdi, A. & Alageel, A. (2021). The Association Between Screen Time Exposure and Autism Spectrum Disorder-Like Symptoms in Children. *Cureus,* 13(10), e18787.

American Psychiatric Association (2013). *Diagnostic and Statistical Manual of Mental Disorders (DSM-5) – 5th Edition.* American Psychiatric Association Publishing.

Aristotle's Rhetoric, Book 2, Chapter 12 in Lee Honeycutt <https://kairos.technorhetoric.net/stasis/2017/honeycutt/aristotle/rhet2-12.html#:~:text=They%20have%20exalted%20notions%2C%20because,that%20means%20having%20exalted%20notions>.

Arnett, J. (1999). Adolescent storm and stress, reconsidered. *American Psychologist*, 54(5), 317–326.

Australian Bureau of Statistics (2018). Household use of information technology. <https://www.abs.gov.au/statistics/industry/technology-and-innovation/household-use-information-technology/latest-release>.

Bandura, A. (1962). *Social Learning through Imitation.* Lincoln, Nebraska: University of Nebraska Press.

Bandura, A. (1977). *Social Learning Theory.* Englewood Cliffs, New Jersey: Prentice Hall.

Bandura, A. & Walters, R. (1963). *Social Learning and Personality Development.* New York: Holt, Rinehart & Winston Inc.

Berninger, V. & Richards, T. (2002). *Brain Literacy for Educators and Psychologists.* New York: Academic Press.

Bjorklund, D. (2005). *Children's Thinking: Cognitive Development and Individual Differences* (4th ed.) Belmont, California: Wadsworth/Thomson Learning.

Blakemore, S. (2008). The social brain in adolescence. *Nature Reviews Neuroscience*, 9(4), 267–277. <https://doi.org/10.1038/nm2353/>.

Borst J., Taatgen, N. & van Rijn, H. (2010). The problem state: a cognitive bottleneck in multitasking. *Journal of Experimental Psychology, Learning, Memory and Cognition*, 36(2), 363–82. <https://doi.org/10.1037/a0018106>.

Bratman, G., Hamilton, J., Hahn, K., Daily, G. & Gross, J. (2015). Nature experience reduces rumination and subgenual prefrontal cortex activation. *Proceedings of the National Academy of Sciences of the United States of America*, 112(28), 8567–8572. <https://doi.org/10.1073/pnas.1510459112>.

Bryson, B. (2019). *The Body: The Guide for Occupants.* London: Doubleday.

Buchholz, K. (2019) How Much of the Internet Consists of Porn? <https://www.statista.com/chart/16959/share-of-the-internet-that-is-porn/#:~:text=Only%204%20percent%20of%20websites,might%20bring%20about%20new%20insights>.
Carr, N. (2011). *The Shallows: What the Internet is Doing to Our Brains.* New York: W.W. Norton & Company.
Carter, R. (2009). *The Human Brain Book: An Illustrated Guide To Its Structure, Function and Disorders.* London: D.K. Publishing.
Child and Youth Mental Health Service, Children's Health Queensland. (June 2014). Submission to the Human Rights Commission's Examination of Intentional Self-harm and Suicidal Behaviour in Children and Young People. <https://humanrights.gov.au/sites/default/files/Submission%20131%20-%20Child%20and%20Youth%20Mental%20Health%20Service,%20Children's%20Health%20Queensland.pdf>.
Corlett, D. & Crabbe, M. (2013). Love and Sex in an Age of Pornography. <https://www.imdb.com/title/tt11496316/>.
Cuzzolin, F., Morelli, A., Cîrstea, B. & Sahakian, B. (2020). Knowing me, Knowing you: Theory of Mind in AI. *Psychological Medicine,* 50, 1057-1061. <https://doi.org/10.1017/S0033291720000835>.
D'angelo, E. (2019). The cerebellum gets social. *Science,* 363(6424), 229. <doi:10.1126/science.aaw2571>.
Dahl, R. (2003). Beyond raging hormones: The tinderbox in the teenage brain. *Cerebrum,* 5(3), 7–22.
Dahl, R. (2004). Adolescent brain development: A period of vulnerabilities or opportunities. *Annals of the New York Academy of Sciences,* 1021(1), 1–22.
Diamond, M. & Hopson, J. (1999). *Magic Trees of the Mind: How to Nurture Your Child's Intelligence, Creativity, and Healthy Emotions from Birth Through Adolescence.* New York: Penguin Putnam Inc.
Durston, S., Davidson, M., Tottenham, N., Galvan, A., Spicer, J., Fossella, J. & Casey, B. (2006). A shift from diffuse to focal cortical activity with development. *Developmental Science,* 9(1), 1–8. <doi.10.1111/j.1467-7687.2005.00454.x>.
Eagleman, D. (2020). *Livewired: The Inside Story of the Ever-Changing Brain.* New York: Pantheon Books.

El-Hamamsy, D., Parmar, C., Shoop-Worrall, S. & Reid, F. (2021) Public understanding of female genital anatomy and pelvic organ prolapse (POP); a questionnaire-based pilot study. *International Urogynecology Journal*, 33, 309–318 (2022). <https://doi.org/10.1007/s00192-021-04727-9>.

Engemann, K., Pedersen, C., Arge, L., Tsirogiannis, C., Mortensen, P. & Svenning, J. (2019). Residential green space in childhood is associated with lower risk of psychiatric disorders from adolescence into adulthood. *Proceedings of the National Academy of Sciences*, 116(11), 5188–5193. <doi.10.3389/neuro.09.031.2009>.

Fried, C. (2008). In-class laptop use and its effects on student learning. *Computers & Education*, 50(3), 906–914.

Gardner, D. (2009). T*he Science of Fear: How the Culture of Fear Manipulates Your Brain*. New York: Plume.

Giedd, J. (2004). Structural magnetic resonance imaging of the adolescent brain. *Annals of the New York Academy of Sciences*, 1021(1), 77–85. <https://doi.org/10.1196/annals.1308.009>.

Giedd, J., Vaituzis, C., Hamburger, S., Lange, N., Rajapakse, J., Kaysen, D., Vauss, Y. & Rapoport, J. (1996). Quantitative MRI of the temporal lobe, amygdala and hippocampus in normal human development: Ages 4–18 years. *Journal of Comparative Neurology*, 366(2), 223–230. <https://doi.org/10.1002/(SICI)1096-9861(19960304)366:2<223::AID-CNE3>3.0.CO;2-7>.

Gold, A. & Toomey, R. (2018). The role of cerebellar impairment in emotion processing: a case study. *Cerebellum Ataxias*, 5(11), 1–9. <doi.org/10.1186/s40673-018-0090-1>.

Hall, G. (1904). *Adolescence: Its Psychology and Its Relations to Physiology, Anthropology, Sociology, Sex, Crime, Religion and Education (Volumes I & II)*. New York: Prentice-Hall.

Harlow, H., Dodsworth, R. & Harlow, M. (1965). Total social isolation in monkeys. *Proceedings of the National Academy of Sciences*, 54(1), 90–97.

Hartig, T., Mitchell, R., de Vries, S. & Frumkin, H. (2014). Nature and Health. A*nnual Review of Public Health*, 35(1), 207–228.

Hattie, J. (2013). *Visible Learning and the Science of How We Learn*. London: Routledge.

Heffler, K., Sienko, D., Subedi, K., McCann, K. & Bennett, D. (2020) Association of Early-Life Social and Digital Media Experiences With Development of Autism Spectrum Disorder–Like Symptoms. *JAMA Pediatrics* 174(7):690–696. <doi:10.1001/jamapediatrics.2020.0230>.

Herculano-Houzel, S. (2009). The human brain in numbers: A linear scaled-up primate brain. *Frontiers in Neuroscience*, 3(31), 1–11.

Herschkowitz, N. & Herschkowitz, E. (2004). *A Good Start to Life: Understanding Your Child's Brain and Behaviour from Birth to Age 6*. New York: Dana Press.

Heying, H. & Weinstein, B. (2021). *A Hunter-Gatherer's Guide to the 21st Century: Evolution and the Challenges of Modern Life*. London: Portfolio/Penguin.

Hill, M. (2014). School ditches rules and loses bullies. <https://www.stuff.co.nz/national/9650581/School-ditches-rules-and-loses-bullies>.

Hirsh-Pasek, K., Zosh, J., Golinkoff, R., Gray, J., Robb, M. & Kaufman, J. (2015). Putting education in 'educational' apps: Lessons from the science of learning. *Psychological Science in the Public Interest*, 16(1), 3–34.

Horvath, M., Alys, L., Massey, K., Pina, A., Scally, M. & Adler, J. (2013). *'Basically... Porn is Everywhere': A Rapid Evidence Assessment on the Effects that Access and Exposure to Pornography has on Children and Young People*. Project Report. Office of the Children's Commissioner for England, London, UK.

Hunter, M., Gillespie, B. & Chen, S. (2019). Urban Nature Experiences Reduce Stress in the Context of Daily Life Based on Salivary Biomarkers. *Frontiers in Psychology*, 10, 722. <https://doi.org/10.3389/fpsyg.2019.00722>.

Kakabadse, A., Kakabadse, N., Bailey, S. & Myers, A. (2009). *Techno Addicts: Young Person Addiction to Technology*. Cambridge: Sigel Press.

Kaplan, S. (1995). The restorative benefits of nature: Toward an integrative framework. *Journal of Environmental Psychology*, 15, 169–182.

Kaplan, R. & Kaplan, S. (1989). *The Experience of Nature: A Psychological Perspective.* Cambridge: Cambridge University Press.

Kim, J., Park, E., Shim, K. & Kim, D. (2018). Hemispherectomy and functional hemispherectomy: Indications and outcomes. *Journal of Epilepsy Research,* 8(1), 1-5.

Korones, S. (2012). Ethiopian kids teach themselves using only tablet computers. <www.zdnet.com/article/ethiopian-kids-teach-themselves-using-only-tablet-computers>.

Kraushaar, J. & Novak, D. (2010). Examining the affects of student multitasking with laptops during the lecture. *Journal of Information Systems Education,* 21(2), 241-251.

LeDoux, J. (1998). *The Emotional Brain: The Mysterious Underpinnings of Emotional Life.* New York: Simon & Schuster Inc.

Lissak, G. (2018). Adverse physiological and psychological effects of screen time on children and adolescents: Literature review and case study. *Environmental Research,* 164, 149-157. <https://doi.org/10.1016/j.envres.2018.01.015>/.

Louv, R. (2008). *Lost Child in the Woods: Saving Our Children from Nature-Deficit Disorder.* Chapel Hill, North Carolina: Algonquin Books of Chapel Hill.

Marengo, D., Longobardi, C., Fabris, M. & Settanni, M. (2018). Highly-visual social media and internalizing symptoms in adolescence: The mediating role of body image concerns. *Computers in Human Behavior,* 82, 63-69. <doi: 10.1016/j.chb.2018.01.003>.

Marston, C. & Lewis, R. (2014) Anal heterosex among young people and implications for health promotion: a qualitative study in the UK. *BMJ Open,* 4:e004996. <doi:10.1136/bmjopen-2014-004996>.

Masten, A., Hubbard, J., Gest, S., Tellegen, A., Garmezy, N. & Ramirez, M. (1999). Competence in the context of adversity: Pathways to resilience and maladaptation from childhood to late adolescence. *Development and Psychopathology,* 11(1), 143-169.

Masten, C., Telzer, E., Fuligni, A., Lieberman, M. & Eisenberger, N. (2012). Time spent with friends in adolescence relates to less neural sensitivity to later peer rejection. *Social Cognitive and Affective Neuroscience,* 7(1), 106-114.

McNicol, M. & Thorsteinsson, E. (2017). Internet addiction, psychological distress, and coping responses among adolescents and adults. *Cyberpsychology, Behavior and Social Networking*, 20(5), 296–304. <https://doi.org/10.1089/cyber.2016.0669>.

Mitchell, K. (2018). *Innate: How the Wiring of Our Brains Shapes Who We Are*. Princeton, New Jersey: Princeton University Press.

Mitchell, K., Finkelhor, D. & Wolak, J. (2003). The exposure of youth to unwanted sexual material on the internet: A national survey of risk, impact, and prevention. *Youth & Society*, 34(3), 330–358. <https://doi.org/10.1177/0044118X02250123>.

Montagni, I., Guichard, E. & Kurth, T. (2016). Association of screen time with self-perceived attention problems and hyperactivity levels in French students: a cross-sectional study. *BMJ Open*, 6(2), e009089. <https://doi.org/10.1136/bmjopen-2015-009089>.

Nagel, M. (2012). *In The Beginning: The Brain, Early Development and Learning*. Melbourne: Australian Council for Educational Research (ACER).

Nagel, M. (2014). I*n the Middle: The Adolescent Brain, Behaviour and Learning*. Melbourne: Australian Council for Educational Research (ACER).

Nagel, M. & Scholes, L. (2016). *Understanding Development and Learning: Implications for Teaching*. Oxford University Press.

Ohly, H., White, M., Wheeler, B., Bethel, A., Ukoumunne, O., Nikolaou, V. & Garside, R. (2016). Attention Restoration Theory: A systematic review of the attention restoration potential of exposure to natural environments. *Journal of toxicology and environmental health. Part B, Critical reviews*, 19(7), 305–343. <https://doi.org/10.1080/10937404.2016.1196155>.

Organisation For Economic Cooperation and Development (OECD) (2015). S*tudents, Computers and Learning: Making the Connection*. Paris, France: OECD Publishing.

Owenz, M. (2021). *Spoiled Right: Delaying Screens and Giving Children What They Really Need*. Amarillo, Texas: Praeclarus Press.

Oz, A. (2001). Big Ideas ABC Television. <https://www.abc.net.au/radionational/programs/archived/radioeye/how-to-cure-a-fanatic---amos-oz/3475244#transcript>.

Pinker, S. (2002). *The Blank Slate: The Modern Denial of Human Nature.* New York: Penguin Books.

Planet Ark. (2011). National Tree Day. 'Climbing Trees: Getting Aussie Kids Back Outdoors'.<https://treeday.planetark.org/documents/doc-534-climbing-trees-research-report-2011-07-13-final.pdf>.

Royal Life Saving Australia. (2020). Royal Life Saving National Drowning Report 2020. Sydney, Australia. <https://www.royallifesaving.com.au/__data/assets/pdf_file/0003/33861/RLS_NationalDrowningReport2020LR-FINAL.pdf>.

Ruder, D. (2008). A work in progress: The teen brain. *Harvard Review*, 3(1), 8-10.

Sales, L. (2021). Bullying on Twitter has become unhinged. It's time to call out the personal, sexist attacks. <https://www.abc.net.au/news/2021-09-14/twitter-social-media-bullies-political-journalism/100458714>.

Sapolsky, R. (2017). *Behave: The Biology of Humans at Our Best and Worst.* New York: Penguin Press.

Sebastian, C., Fontaine, N., Bird, G., Blakemore, S., De Brito, S., McCrory, E. & Viding, E. (2012). Neural processing associated with cognitive and affective Theory of Mind in adolescents and adults. *Social Cognitive and Affective Neuroscience*, 7(1), 53-63. <https://doi.org/10.1093/scan/nsr023>.

Shamay-Tsoory, S., Harari, H., Aharon-Peretz, J. & Levkovitz, Y. (2010). The role of the orbitofrontal cortex in affective theory of mind deficits in criminal offenders with psychopathic tendencies. *Cortex*, 46(5), 668-677. <doi.10.1016/j.cortex.2009.04.008>.

Shanahan, D., Bush, R., Gaston, K., Lin, B., Dean, J., Barber, E. & Fuller, R. (2016). Health Benefits from Nature Experiences Depend on Dose. *Scientific Reports*, 6, 28551. <https://doi.org/10.1038/srep28551>.

Sigman, A. (2009). Well connected?: The biological implications of 'social networking'. *The Biologist*, 56(1), 14-20.

Snell, T., Lam, J., Lau, W. W., Lee, I., Maloney, E., Mulholland, N., Wilson, L. & Wynne, L. (2016). Contact with Nature in Childhood and Adult Depression. *Children, Youth and Environments*, 26(1), 111-124. <https://doi.org/10.7721/chilyoutenvi.26.1.0111>.

Soga, M. & Gaston, K. (2016). Extinction of experience: The loss of human–nature interactions. *Frontiers in Ecology and the Environment* 14(2) 94–101. <doi:10.1002/fee.1225>.

Spring, M. (2021). Frances Haugen says Facebook is 'making hate worse'. <https://www.bbc.com/news/technology-59038506>.

Steinberg, L., Dahl, R., Keating, D., Kupfer, D., Masten, A. & Pine, D. (2006). The study of developmental psychopathology in adolescence: Integrating affective neuroscience with the study of context. In D. Cicchetti & D. J. Cohen, (Eds.), *Developmental Psychopathology, Vol 2:* Developmental neuroscience, 2nd ed., (pp. 710–741). Hoboken, New Jersey: John Wiley & Sons Inc.

Stoodley, C. (2016). The cerebellum and neurodevelopmental disorders. *Cerebellum*, 15(1), 34–37. <doi:10.1007/s12311-015-0715-3>.

Sugata, M., Dangwal, R., Chatterjee, S., Jha, S., Bisht, R. & Kapur, P. (2005). Acquisition of computer literacy on shared public computers: Children and the 'hole in the wall'. *Australasian Journal of Educational Technology*, 21(3), 407–426.

Sweeney, M. (2009). *Brain, The Complete Guide: How It Develops, How It Works and How To Keep It Sharp.* Washington, DC: National Geographic Society.

The Sydney Playground Project (2017). <https://www.sydneyplaygroundproject.com/>.

Tankard-Reist, M. (2019) *Submission to the House of Representatives Standing Committee on Social Policy and Legal Affairs Inquiry into Age Verification for Online Wagering and Online Pornography.* Submission 177 at <https://www.aph.gov.au/Parliamentary Business/Committees/House/Social Policy and Legal Affairs/Online>.

Taylor, A. & Kuo, F. (2008). Children with attention deficits concentrate better after walk in the park. *Journal of Attention Disorders*, 12(5), 402–409.

Tester-Jones, M., White, M., Elliott, L., Weinstein, N., Grellier, J., Economou, T., Bratman, G., Cleary, A., Gascon, M., Korpela, K., Nieuwenhuijsen, M., O'Connor, A., Ojala, A., van den Bosch, M. & Fleming, L. (2020). Results from an 18 country cross-sectional study examining experiences of nature for people with common mental health disorders. *Scientific Reports,* 10(1), 19408, <doi.org/10.1038/s41598-020-75825-9>.

Twenge, J. (2017). *iGen: Why Today's Super-Connected Kids are Growing Up Less Rebellious, More Tolerant, Less Happy and Completely Unprepared for Adulthood.* New York: Atria Books.

Twenge, J., Joiner, T., Rogers, M., & Martin, G. (2018). Increases in depressive symptoms, suicide-related outcomes, and suicide rates among U.S. adolescents after 2010 and links to increased new media screen time. *Clinical Psychological Science,* 6(1), 3–17. <https://doi.org/10.1177/2167702617723376>.

Uhls, Y., Michikyan, M., Morris, J., Garcia, D., Small, G., Zgourou, E. & Greenfield, P. (2014). Five days at outdoor education camp without screens improves preteen skills with nonverbal emotion cues. *Computers and Human Behavior,* 39, 387–392.

Ulrich, R. (1984). View through a window may influence recovery from surgery. *Science,* 224(4647), 420–421.

Ulrich, R. (1983). Aesthetic and affective response to natural environment. In I. Altman, & J.F. Wohlwill (Eds). *Human Behavior and Environment – Volume 6* (pp. 85-125). New York: Plenum Press.

Ulrich, R., Simons, R., Losito, B., Fiorito, E., Miles, M. & Zelson, M. (1991). Stress recovery during exposure to natural and urban environments. *Journal of Environmental Psychology,* 11, 201–230.

Vannucci, A., Flannery, K., & Ohannessian, C. (2017). Social media use and anxiety in emerging adults. *Journal of Affective Disorders,* 207, 163–166. <doi.org/10.1016/j.jad.2016.08.040>.

Voss, P., Thomas, M., Cisneros-Franco, J. & de Villers-Sidani, E. (2017). Dynamic brains and the changing rules of neuroplasticity: Implications for learning and recovery. *Frontiers in Psychology,* 8:1657. <doi.10.3389/fpsyg.2017.01657>.

Ward Thompson, C., Aspinall, P., Roe, J., Robertson, L. & Miller, D. (2016). Mitigating Stress and Supporting Health in Deprived Urban Communities: The Importance of Green Space and the Social Environment. *International Journal of Environmental Research and Public Health.* 13(4):440. <https://doi.org/10.3390/ijerph13040440>.

Weimer, A., Parault Dowds, S., Fabricius, W., Schwanenflugel, P. & Suh, G. (2017). Development of constructivist theory of mind from middle childhood to early adulthood and its relation to social cognition and behavior. *Journal of Experimental Child Psychology*, 154, 28–45. <https://doi.org/10.1016/j.jecp.2016.10.002>.

White, M., Alcock, I., Grellier, J., Wheeler, B., Hartig, T., Warber, S., Bone, A., Depledge, M. & Fleming, L. (2019). Spending at least 120 minutes a week in nature is associated with good health and wellbeing. *Scientific Reports,* 9, 7730. <https://doi.org/10.1038/s41598-019-44097-3>.

Wilbrecht, L. (2018). Your twelve-year-old isn't just sprouting new hair but is also forming (and being formed by) new neural connections. In D. J. Linden (Ed.), *Think Tank: Forty Neuroscientists Explore the Roots of Human Experience* (pp. 45–51). New Haven, Connecticut: Yale University Press.

Wood, E., Zivcakova, L., Gentile, P., Archer, K., De Pasquale, D. & Nosk, A. (2011). Examining the impact of off-task multi-tasking with technology on real-time classroom learning. *Computers & Education*, 58(1), 365–374.

Zach, A., Meyer, N., Hendrowarsito, L., Kolb, S., Bolte, G., Nennstiel-Ratzel, U., Stilianakis, N., Herr, C. & GME Study Group (2016). Association of sociodemographic and environmental factors with the mental health status among preschool children-Results from a cross-sectional study in Bavaria, Germany. *International Journal of Hygiene and Environmental Health*, 219(4–5), 458–467. <https://doi.org/10.1016/j.ijheh.2016.04.012>.

Index

academic outcomes 44–48
academic skills 44–48, 52
addiction 61, 64, 68–69
adolescence 20, 23–35
adolescent brain 4, 11, 20, 26–27, 30, 34
adolescent development 4
age 22
aggression 33
alcohol 32
American Psychiatric Association 50, 68
amygdala 30–31, 33
anal sex 73–74
Anderson, Thomas 38
anger 33

Ansari, Aziz 75–76
anticipatory dopamine 56
anxiety 26, 78, 104
anxiety disorders 12, 80
Apple 39–40
apps 6, 40, 44–45
Aristotle 26, 88
Armstrong, Neil 66
attention 13
Attention Deficit Hyperactivity Disorder (ADHD) 58, 103–105
Attention Restoration Theory (ART) 102–103
attention span 54
Australian Bureau of Statistics 66

Autism Spectrum Disorder (ASD) 12, 18, 59, 91, 98, 112
autistic-like behaviours 4, 89–90, 103, 109, 112
autistification 6, 87–98
autonomy 61, 106
axon 17

baby boomer 2, 63, 74
Bachchan, Amitabh 77
behaviour 13, 82–83
Behavioural Activation Theory 82–83, 98
biophilia 101
bipolar illness 18
borrowed power 81, 83
body language 90
brain 2, 4, 10, 11, 19–20, 75
brain stem 11–13, 30
Brexit 93
bring your own device 41
bullying 69–70, 85–86, 106

Carr, Nicholas 1
cerebellum 11–13
cerebrum 13–14, 30
Child and Youth Mental Health Service (CYMHS) 71
childhood obesity 61
classical conditioning 72
COBOL 39
cognitive bottleneck 49
cold turkey 64
competence 61, 105–106
concentration 2, 15, 27, 54, 58, 96
contextual autism 6
COVID-19 81, 113

cry-bully 84, 86, 96
cults 82
cyberbullying 69–71
cybersex 71–75

Dahl, Ronald 23
death grip 72–73
decision-making 15, 25, 27–28, 32–35, 106
depression 108
desensitisation 67–68, 73
Diagnostic and Statistical Manual (DSM) 50, 68
Diamond, Marian 9
digital education revolution (DER) 45
ding 56–58, 62
distraction 49, 55, 58, 62, 64
dopamine 31–32, 34, 56, 83, 90
Dr Seuss 97
drowning 57
drugs 32, 68
dyslexia 12, 18

Eagleman, David 20
eating disorders 80
e-learning 3
emotion 13, 15, 28–30
environment 99, 112
epidemic 111
Ethiopia 43
evolutionary psychology 103, 112
executive functions 15
experience-dependent 16–18
experience-expectant 16–18
experiences 15–18, 20, 30
extremist 95, 97

Facebook 40, 69, 79, 85, 88, 92
fanatic 87, 96
fear of missing out (FOMO) 69, 81, 84
fight-or-flight 11, 20, 33
Flickr 40
FORTRAN 39–40
frontal lobes 14–15, 27–28, 54, 79

gambling games 56
gaming 3, 68
Gardner, Daniel 111
gender dysphoria 80
Gillard, Julia 45
glial cells 10
Google 57, 78

Hall, G. Stanley 26
Harlow, Harry 101
Haugen, Frances 92
headlines 58, 60
health issue 3–4
hemispherectomy 21–22
Heying, Heather 6
hippocampus 13
homework 51, 69
Hopson, Janet 9
hormones 4, 13, 25–26, 32
Human Rights Commission 71

identity development 82, 98
impulses 27, 34
information and computer technology (ICT) 41–48, 51
Instagram 40, 69, 79, 83, 85
intermittent reinforcement 56, 63, 68

internet addiction 50
intimacy-building 92, 95
intuition 27
Invisible Gorilla Experiment 55
iPad 40
isolation 50

Jensen, Frances 28
Jobs, Steve 39
judgement 15, 27, 77

King Jr, Martin Luther 97

labiaplasty 72, 79
language 27, 39, 45, 95
learning deficits 45
LeDoux, Joseph 10
left-handedness 18
Leunig, Michael 57
limbic system 12–13, 28, 31, 33
lockdown 50, 63–64
logic 27
Louv, Richard 99

marketing 41, 55, 98
mathematical literacy 46, 54
maturation 4, 20, 23, 29
media studies 3
#MeToo 75
melatonin 51
meltdown 64
memory 13, 19, 49, 51–52, 55
mental health 6, 48, 64, 68–69, 78, 105, 113
Microsoft 40
millennials 40, 63, 88, 94
Miller, Jody 21–22

mindset 3
Minister for Loneliness 92
Mitra, Sugata 43
modelling 63
motivation 13, 28, 32
multi-tasking 49, 52
myelin 16–18, 29–30

narcissism 92, 98
natural environment 99, 100–102 104–108
natural selection 112
nature 16, 26, 34, 90, 99–109
Nature Deficit Disorder 104
Navratilova, Martina 59–60
Negroponte, Nicholas 43–44
Neo (*The Matrix*) 37–38, 52
neural connectivity 16
neurons 10, 12, 17, 19–20, 29–30, 39, 88, 91
neuroplasticity 4, 18–22
neurotransmitters 10, 32, 56
New Delhi 43
NIIT 43
nipple-resizing 72
notifications 58
nucleus accumbens 30–32, 34
nurture 16–17, 34

O'Hara, Scarlett 78
object permanence 54
obsessive-compulsive disorder 2
occipital lobes 14
One Laptop Per Child 43–44
Organisation for Economic Co-operation and Development (OECD) 45–47

overuse 3, 45, 49–50
Oz, Amos 95–97

parietal lobes 14
Parker, Peter 100
Parkinson's disease 32
passive-aggressive 70, 85–86
peer norms 67
Pentium 40
personality 27
physical activity 61, 105
plasticity 18–19
play 44, 61, 89, 105–109
popularity 81, 83–84, 98
pornography 71–75
prefrontal lobes 28, 34–35
Programme for International Student Assessment (PISA) 46
psychiatric disorders 105
puberty 22, 25, 51, 59, 89

reading literacy 46–47
red pill 5
rewards 28, 30–31, 33, 56
risk-taking 32, 106, 108
Rudd, Kevin 45
rumination 69, 108

Sales, Leigh 85
schizophrenia 12, 32
Schleicher, Andreas 46
scientific literacy 46
screen devices 3, 6, 42, 47, 50, 61–64
screen time 50, 61–62, 104
screen usage 6, 61–64

screenager 30, 64
seizures 21
self-harm 80
sex hormones 25
sex segregation 60
sexuality 65, 75
Silicon Valley 2, 109
Skinner, B. F. 31
sleep 13, 49, 51–52, 61–63
sleep deprivation 27, 51–52
sleep disturbance 49, 51
smartphone 40, 43, 58, 66, 70
social comparision 78–79
social contagion 80–81
social disease 5
social exclusion 78
Social Learning Theory 67
social media 3, 5, 40, 49, 51, 66–70, 77–86, 92, 94–98, 108
social skills 75, 89–90
stress 26, 74, 104, 108
Stress Recovery Theory (SRT) 102–103
suicide 70, 78
Sydney Playground Project 106
synaptic connections 19, 30

tantrum 63–64
temperament 27
temporal lobes 14
The Matrix 5, 37–38, 59
Theory of Mind (ToM) 28–29, 59–60, 67, 72, 75–76, 94
tobacco 58
Tolstoy, Leo 53
Tourette's syndrome 32
transgender 59–60

trans-exclusionary radical feminist (TERF) 59
Triandis, Harry 95
trolling 70, 85
tweets 58
Twitter 40, 85–86

Uhls, Yalda 90
Ulrich, Roger 102

violence 65–68, 72–73
virginity 71
virtual world 5–6, 30, 34–35, 38, 75, 96, 102, 108

Weinstein, Bret 6
wellbeing 2, 6, 26, 31–32, 41, 48–50, 61, 69, 90, 102, 105–106, 108
wi-fi 40
Wolf, Naomi 65
working memory 55
World Ruby Union 60
Wozniak, Steve 39

YouTube 40

www.ingramcontent.com/pod-product-compliance
Lightning Source LLC
Chambersburg PA
CBHW070108120526
44588CB00032B/1383